Shyh-ming Lin
Fu-ren Lin

Integrated Multi-Agent Systems for Coordinating Mobile Activities

Shyh-ming Lin
Fu-ren Lin

Integrated Multi-Agent Systems for Coordinating Mobile Activities

金琅学术出版社

Impressum / 出版事项
Bibliografische Information der Deutschen Nationalbibliothek: Die Deutsche Nationalbibliothek verzeichnet diese Publikation in der Deutschen Nationalbibliografie; detaillierte bibliografische Daten sind im Internet über http://dnb.d-nb.de abrufbar.

德意志国家图书馆出版的文献目录信息：德意志国家图书馆在德意志国家图书目录上发布了该出版物;详细的文献数据可在因特网http://dnb.d-nb.de 上获得。

Coverbild / 封面图片: www.ingimage.com

Verlag / 出版社:
Golden Light Academic Publishing / 金琅学术出版社
ist ein Imprint der OmniScriptum GmbH & Co. KG /
是属于 OmniScriptum GmbH & Co. KG的注册商标
Bahnhofstr 26, 66111 Saarbrücken, Deutschland /
德国，萨尔布吕肯市，Heinrich-Böcking-Str. 6-8，邮编 66121
Email / 电子邮箱: info@omniscriptum.com

Herstellung: siehe letzte Seite /
印刷: 见末页
ISBN / 国际标准书号: 978-3-330-82027-2

Zugl. / 批准者 : Kaohsiung, National Sun Yat-sen University, Phd thesis, 2007

Integrated Multi-agent Systems for Coordinating Mobile Activities

Shyh-ming Lin
Fu-ren Lin

Abstract

As mobile communication services get more and more pervasively available, it becomes increasingly convenient for people to interact with the world. With mobile devices, people can easily plan and run their activity schedules. Also, since mobile users can instantly perceive contextual information, they are likely to adjust their objectives and decision makings as the environmental context varies. That is, their activity schedules tend to be context-dependent. Should anything unexpected happen, a mobile user is apt to adapt their activity schedule to reduce the impact. However, since the environmental resources in the mobile environment are limited and therefore cannot satisfy all users' demands, schedule clashes or conflicts are inevitable. We concentrate on resolving the conflicts, which are formulated as a Multi-objective Context-dependent Distributed Constraint Optimization Problem (MCDCOP). The problem is complicated and highly dynamic, and the joint optimality to the problem might be time-variant. We propose an integrated multi-agent system SPA and a novel problem-solving approach 2S-DORA to facilitate the coordination of mobile users' activities to maintain optimality. The SPA, which integrates the Simulated and Physical Agents, is employed to enhance mobile users' sensory, analytic, reasoning and social abilities. The 2S-DORA, a Two Stage Distributed Optimality Reaching Approach, takes advantage of the SPA to help mobile users quickly and effectively adapt themselves to the context variations and exceptions. We take a traveling backpacker problem as an example and conducted five experiments to demonstrate how the SPA+2S-DORA contribute to solving the MCDCOP.

Keywords: multi-objective context-dependent DCOP; distributed constraint optimization problem; simulated agents; physical agents; mobile environment; flexible coordination mechanism

Table of Contents

List of Symbols

B1	a backpacker without any communication mobile device
B2	a backpacker with a pure mobile device
B3	a backpacker with a SPA+2S-DORA embedded mobile device
D	discrete value domain of a variable
F	the total cost
MU	a set of N mobile users
N^+	the domain of positive natural number
T	the time length
P	the preferences of a mobile user
R	the domain of real numbers
R^+	the domain of positive real number
S	the features and conditions of a service provider
SP	a set of M service providers
V	a set of variables
X	a set of variables controlled by an agent
a	an agent
c	a cost
context	the environmental context
$\mathrm{sp}_i.\mathrm{cur}_p$	the capacity utilization rate of pth cycle of ith tourist attraction
dist(A, B)	a distance function that measures the distance from A to B
ec	an expected cost
es	an expected satisfaction
eu	an expected utility
f	an objective (cost) function
g	an equality constraint
h	an inequality constraint
mu	a mobile user
p	a preference function, preference order number

p	the cycle no.
s	the starting time of a service cycle
sp	a service provider
state	the immediate state of a mobile user
t	time
t_c	a random generated time period
u	a utility
v	the average moving speed of a mobile user
w_c	the importance (weighting) of the cost
w_u	the importance (weighting) of the utility
x	a variable
x	the x coordinate
y	the y coordinate
Π	a mobile user's initial position
Π_t	a mobile user's instant position
Φ	the relations between mobile users and service providers
β	the coefficient of the sigmoid function for the cost-satisfaction model
χ	the capacity
δ	the service cycle time
η	the geographical location
$\varphi_{p,j}$	the relation between the mobile user j and the pth service cycle of a specific service provider
$\kappa_{A,B}$	the cost and time required while moving from A to B
π	a mobile user's policy (schedule)
π^*	an optimal policy (schedule)
π^-	the fulfilled part of an optimal policy (schedule)
θ	the percentage of tickets reserved for locale backpackers
ρ	the ratio of backpackers who carries the SPA+2S-DORA embedded mobile devices

τ	a specific service provider
$\tau_{r,m}$	the mth cycle of a specific service provider, which is a mobile users' r^{th} desired activity
$\succ$	the preference order, greater than

List of Figures

List of Tables

Integrated Multi-agent Systems for Coordinating Mobile Activities

Chapter 1 Introduction

1.1 Overview

The rapid advances in information technology and telecommunication along with the explosive growth of web accessible services have allowed people to access instant information and request services anytime and everywhere. Nowadays, a large majority of people are tightly coupled with computers when they are engaged in their daily activities. Weiser in 1991 first called it the ubiquitous computing. The ubiquitous computing (or mobile computing) enables the computing and communication services to surround people anytime and everywhere. The mobile computing has been evolving new applications, new services, and new business models.

In a mobile communication environment, mobile users and service providers are key players. A mobile user is an individual equipped with a computation and wireless device moves around a domain where wireless infrastructure has been established and ready for use. Therefore, while engaging in their activities, any mobile user can access information or interact anytime with the other mobile users or service providers. Through interaction, instant contextual information can be continuously shared, conveyed or accessed.

The information used to characterize a player's situation is the player's context (Dey & Abowd, 1999). In a mobile environment, mobile users' contexts vary as time advances. Kramer, Modsching, Hagen, and Gretzel (2007) found that users of electronic tour guides were very likely to alter their itinerary during their travels. Wang, Park, and Fesenmaier (2012) indicated that the instant information gathered through mobile devices led travelers to re-plan their activities so as to enjoy more services and richer experiences. That is, by learning the time-variant context, more and more mobile users take updated contextual information into consideration while developing policies, making decisions and taking action. To maximize personal satisfaction, they tend to change their goals in response to the environmental dynamics. The tendency, which causes the mobile environment to be increasingly dynamic and complicated, contributes to an emerging problem. That is, conflicts or crashes arise while mobile users are planning, modifying policies or handling the unexpected circumstances. Besides, the dynamics increase service providers' difficulty in delivering services during the process of user consumption (O'Grady & O'Hare, 2005). In a mobile environment, Niemelä and Latvakoski (2004) suggested that advanced services are required for dynamic resource management and optimal coordination. The coordination among mobile users is necessary, and we call it Mobile Users Coordination Problem (MUCP).

In an MUCP, we characterize the mobile users as follows. (1) They are independent and self-interested. (2) They share constraints with related ones. (3) Their objectives are context-dependent. The context is time-variant. (4) They frequently enter or leave the environment. (5) They are temporarily connected when coordinating with others. Accordingly, we formulate the MUCP as a Multi-objective Context-dependent Distributed Constraint Optimization Problem (MCDCOP), where mobile users are loosely-coupled and maintain only short-term inter-relations. The MCDCOP is a problem in which more than one mobile user is involved in optimizing individual objectives and policies (i.e., schedules to enjoy desired activities) subject to shared constraints. Moreover, some are likely to adjust their objectives or policies once the environmental contexts vary or any exception happens. Briefly, the MCDCOP is a distributed constraint optimization problem; its goals are multiple, distributed, context-dependent and time-variant.

We aim to resolve the conflicts that are likely to occur in a mobile environment. To achieve this goal, we propose a new framework SPA, and a novel problem-solving approach 2S-DORA. The SPA, which integrates Simulated and

Physical Agents, enhances mobile users' abilities in detection, analysis, inference and social interaction. Physical agents in SPA detect the variation of social situations, invoke simulated agents to simulate and infer when necessary, offer help to mobile users with their activity schedules, and coordinate with other physical agents. Simulated agents build mobile users' cognitive structure of the environment based on the information gathered by physical agents, run simulations corresponding to the social situations, and then support physical agents in making decisions.

The 2S-DORA, which is the abbreviation of Two Stage Distributed Optimality Reaching Approach, can real-time and online support solution quality improvement for the MCDCOP. The first stage of 2S-DORA is the self-planning stage, and the second the cooperative improvement stage. At the self-planning stage, the 2S-DORA helps the distributed mobile users plan their personal activity schedules subject to the shared constraints. Thereafter at the cooperative improvement stage, the 2S-DORA enables users to improve personal schedules so as to approach a joint optimality. The idea of the 2S-DORA at its cooperative improvement stage is that for a mobile user who wants to improve his/her personal activity schedule, s/he can initialize a temporary coordination network to exchange his/her activity reservation with other users. Through the exchanges, which follow the premises of social exchange theory and Pareto improvement, mobile users can jointly obtain their optimal schedules. The exchanges can enable mobile users to handle conflicts, context variations or exceptions. We implement the 2S-DORA on the SPA framework. With the SPA+2S-DORA embedded mobile devices, users are able to coordinate with the others to always maintain the optimality.

We elaborate a traveling backpacker problem, which is an extension of the MUCP, as an example to demonstrate how the SPA+2S-DORA contribute to the conflict resolution caused by context variations and exceptions. Backpackers, public transportation, and tourist attractions are major players in the problem. A traveling backpacker is an independent traveler who plans his/her own itinerary and wanders in the mobile environment. The public transportation transports backpackers from one location to another desired location. The tourist attractions bring joy and fun to the backpackers. In the problem, every backpacker pursues his/her own goal. A conflict, which occurs once any tourist attraction is fully booked up and additional bookings cannot be accepted, will constrain a backpacker's schedule. Furthermore, such a context as weather condition or an exception as traffic congestion can affect backpackers' schedules and their decisions.

The traveling backpacker problem is an MCDCOP, and the proposed SPA+2S-DORA are applied to solve the problem. We finally design and conduct five experiments to observe and evaluate the performance of the SPA+2S-DORA on the traveling backpacker problem.

1.2 Motivation and Objective

We are motivated by the awareness of demands to resolve the frequently arising conflicts on utilizing resources among mobile users. In the environment, all users pursue their personal objectives; the circumstances are dynamic and complicated. Constraints, which lead to conflicts, are shared among mobile users.

The conflict resolution in the mobile environment is a critical issue. The scarcity of environmental resources explains why conflicts occur. For instance, conflicts will arise when the capacity of a service provider is full, and additional demands from consumers cannot be accepted. The conflicts are likely to occur when mobile users are planning, adapting or altering their activity schedules. Traditional coordination techniques cannot handle such conflicts because the mobile users maintain only short-term inter-relations and the conflicts are dynamic and distributed.

Our objective is to propose valid techniques to solve the emerging problem concerning the distributed conflicts in the mobile environment. We analyze why conflicts occur and what the characteristics of conflicts are, and try to figure out a systematic and intelligent approach for mobile users to resolve their conflicts.

1.3 Solving MUCP

We formulate the MUCP as an MCDCOP. To solve this problem, we propose an approach which synthesizes the following two main elements:

1. *Integrated multi-agent systems* (*SPA*): The SPA utilizes the corresponding capabilities of simulated and physical agents, combines the analytic and reasoning abilities of simulated agents and the sensory and social abilities of physical agents. Swarm serves as the example of a simulated agent platform, and JADE as that of a physical agent platform. Both platforms are java-based and thus can be integrated to cooperate with each other. The SPA can enable mobile users to not only make decisions after having sufficient consideration but also remotely interact with the others. The SPA can operate in the distributed environment and interoperate with other SPAs.
2. *Two Stage Distributed Optimality Reaching Approach* (*2S-DORA*): At its first stage, the 2S-DORA employs a forward chaining method to enable mobile users to plan their personal activity schedules subject to the environmental constraints. At the second stage, the 2S-DORA offers a flexible coordination mechanism, a communication language, and a reservation exchange protocol. The mechanism enables the conflict-related mobile users to form temporary coordination network. The language facilitates users' communication. The protocol regulates the improvement of activity schedules.

1.4 Assumption and Limitation

The assumptions and limitations are listed as follows.

1. The mobile users are those who can access mobile network to interact both with each other and with service providers anytime and everywhere.
2. The mobile environment is distributed. No one in the environment owns complete information.
3. A mobile user, who employs SPA+2S-DORA, carries a GPS embedded mobile device. The GPS can sense its owner's instant position.
4. Every mobile user is rational. They pursue their maximum satisfaction subject to constraints.
5. All service providers are capacity-limited and provide services according to

their timetables.

6. The service providers do not actively promote their services.
7. Every mobile user, under the condition that their self-interests won't be sacrificed, is willing to help the others improve their satisfaction with their schedules.
8. The mobile users consider transportation costs when moving from one position to another. The costs are proportional to the distance between two positions.
9. The mobile users neglect their communication costs when interacting with others using mobile devices.
10. The service providers do not charge for their services.

1.5 Organization of the Remaining Chapters

We organize the remaining chapters as follows. Chapter 2 reviews the related works. Chapter 3 cites a simplified example to demonstrate the MUCP. Chapter 3 abstractly formulates the MUCP into an MCDCOP and derives the requirements to solve the problem. Chapter 4 elucidates the framework of SPA and how the integrated multi-agent systems operate and interoperate. Chapter 5 develops a systematic and intelligent approach, the 2S-DORA. Chapter 6 elaborates an example of the traveling backpacker problem, models the problem and explains how the SPA+2S-DORA support mobile activities coordination. Chapter 7 designs five experiments to evaluate the performance of the SPA+2S-DORA. Chapter 8 conducts the experiments and discusses the experimental results. Chapter 9 concludes and proposes some future research directions.

Chapter 2 Related Works

This chapter reviews the technologies and literature regarding the problem formulation and the problem-solving technique. We organize this chapter as follows. First of all, Section 2.1 reviews the multi-agent technologies, which are applied to resolving the conflict problems in the mobile environment. Section 2.2 introduces the multi-objective optimization problem and the definition of the optimum conditions to this kind of problem. Section 2.3 introduces the DCOP, which is extended to model our MUCP in Chapter 3. Moreover, this section surveys various extended DCOPs and the techniques for solving them. Section 2.4 reviews the agent-based coordination mechanisms for Chapter 5 to propose a suitable coordination mechanism structure. Section 2.5 introduces the cases of the scheduling problems and traveling salesman problems for Chapter 3 to model players' behaviors of the MUCP. Section 2.6 introduces the computational intelligence. Section 2.7 reviews the forward chaining method for Chapter 5 to design our 2S-DORA. Section 2.8 reviews Pareto improvement and methods that help distributed optimization problem converge to global optimality. We apply them to designing the 2S-DORA in Chapter 5.

2.1 Multi-agent Technologies

The integrated multi-agent systems (SPA) are developed based on the multi-agent technologies. Agents are intelligent software programs that serve as personal assistants to perform certain duties.

Agents are autonomous, proactive, and adaptive software that can perform complicated tasks autonomously to solve a growing number of complex problems (Foner, 1993; Hayes-Roth, 1995; Maes, 1995; 1991; Wooldridge & Jennings, 1995). Besides, agents contain some level of intelligence, from fixed rules to learning engines that allow them to adapt to changes in the environment (Krause et al., 1997). Russell and Norvig (2003) thought that an agent is not merely a software program. Russell and Norvig further completely characterized the agent as follows: an agent operates under autonomous control, perceives their environment, persists over a prolonged time period, adapts to change and is capable of taking on another's goals.

An agent is rational if it acts to maximize its utility; however, its behavior in achieving given goals is imposed by given conditions and constraints, which is coined as the bounded rationality (Simon, 1982). Framing the MUCP with the concept of bounded rationality, the coherence of plans scheduled by different players may be constrained by incomplete information, information processing costs, and some non-neoclassical objective functions of economic models.

A multi-agent system is a combinatorial software system that is made up of more than one agent. In a multi-agent environment, agents can either cooperate with other agents to carry out a common duty or compete with the other agents to pursue their own interests. Durfee and Lesser (1989) defined the multi-agent system as a loosely coupled network of problem solvers that interact to solve problems that are beyond the individual capabilities or knowledge of each problem solver. Jennings et al. (1998) identified the characteristics of multi-agent systems as: (1) each agent has incomplete capabilities to solve a problem; (2) system control is distributed; (3) data is decentralized; (4) computation is asynchronous.

Though the multi-agent technology can be applied to solve complicated problems by decomposing them into several simple sub-problems, there are many challenges researchers have to face while they are designing or implementing multi-agent systems. These challenges are the domain specification, communication coordination, computational, implementation, and verification problems (Oliveira, Fischer, & Stepankova, 1999).

The multi-agent technologies nowadays are broadly applied to many fields, including biology, sociology, economics, organization and management science, complex systems, and philosophy (Oliveira et al., 1999). Among these applications of agent technologies, there are basically two types of agent designs: *simulated* and *physical* agents. Simulated agents capture the structure of individuals, including the individuals' mental states (beliefs, desires, and intentions) (Weiss, 1999) and their corresponding decision models, and then simulate and analyze their interactions. An agent-based simulation model is developed based on three research areas, including agent-based computing, social sciences, and computer simulation (Davidsson, 2002). Physical agents, on behalf of individuals, can communicate, coordinate, and collaborate with corresponding physical agents representing other individuals. Physical agents can interact with each other in a physical environment without boundary.

The characteristics described here show that multi-agent technologies have great potential to support mobile activities coordination. The multi-agent systems embedded in mobile devices can help mobile users plan their personal schedules, gather information from the mobile environment, exchange information and negotiate with other users to resolve possible occurring conflicts.

2.2 Multi-objective Optimization Problem

Different from a single objective optimization problem, a multi-objective optimization problem aims at simultaneously optimizing more than one objective. To solve a multi-objective optimization problem is to find a number of Pareto-optimal solutions, rather than find a single globally optimal solution. Pareto-optimality, named after Vilfredo Pareto, is the outcome of a game under the condition that there is no other outcome that makes every player at least as well off and at least one player strictly better off (http://www.gametheory.net/Dictionary/ParetoOptimal.html). A typical multi-objective optimization problem is expressed as follows (Rao, 1991):

Minimize/Maximize $f_i(x)$ i=1,2,...,N

Subject to

$g_j(x) = 0$ $\quad$ j=1,2,..., J

$h_k(x) \leq 0$ $\quad$ k=1,2,..., K,

where $f_i(x)$ is the ith objective, and $g_j(x)$ and $h_k(x)$ are respectively the jth and k^{th} interdependent equality and inequality constraints. The multi-objective optimization problems so far investigated in engineering and economics fields are mostly centralized problems. In a centralized multi-objective optimization problem, all variables and constraints are controlled and objectives are evaluated in a centralized environment.

The Pareto optimality E and weak Pareto optimality WE are defined as follows (T'Kindt & Billaut, 2002):

> Pareto optimality E: *Consider K conflicting criteria* Z_i *to be minimized.* $\boldsymbol{S}$ *is the set of solutions and* $\boldsymbol{Z}$ *its image in the criteria space.* $x \in S$ *is a Pareto optimum (or an efficient solution) iff* $\neg\exists y \in S$, $x \neq y$, *such that* $Z_i(y) \leq Z_i(x)$, $\forall i$, $i=1,\ldots,K$, *with at least one strict inequality. E is the set of all Pareto optima and* $\boldsymbol{Z}_E$ *its image in the criteria space.*

> Weak Pareto optimality WE: *Consider K conflicting criteria* Z_i *to be minimized.* $\boldsymbol{S}$ *is the set of solutions and* $\boldsymbol{Z}$ *its image in the criteria space.* $x \in S$ *is a weak Pareto optimum (or a weak efficient solution) iff* $\neg\exists y \in S$, $x \neq y$, *such that* $Z_i(y) < Z_i(x)$, $\forall i$, $i=1,\ldots,K$. *WE is the set of all Pareto optima and* $\boldsymbol{Z}_{WE}$ *its image in the criteria space. One has* $E \subseteq WE$.

Compared with the centralized multi-objective optimization problem, there is little research focused on the distributed multi-objective optimization problem. Wang (2001), Wittner et al. (2002) and Bui et al.,(2006) systematically decomposed the large scale and complex multi-objective optimization problem into several layered hierarchical sub-optimization problems, distributed the sub-problems in the parallel and distributed computing environment, and used evolutionary techniques to solve this problem. The objective of the decomposition is to reduce the requirement of computation resource and time. The decomposition heavily relies on experts' domain knowledge. Moreover, the hierarchy of the optimization problem must be fixed. The problem-solving techniques for multi-objective optimization problems proposed up to now cannot handle such a dynamic problem as the multi-objective context-dependent DCOP that arises in the mobile environment.

2.3 DCOP and Techniques for Solving DCOP

Distributed Constraint Optimization Problem, abbreviated as DCOP, is a problem in which variables and constraints are distributed among all the involved agents. To solve a DCOP is to find a set of values for variables to not only consistently satisfy the inter-agent constraints but also optimize agents' common objective functions. One major difference between a DOCP and a general constraint problem is that in a DOCP, no agent has an overall view of the whole problem, and every agent maintains merely its own agent view. Therefore, the optimal solution can only be obtained through agents' message exchange and distributed optimization techniques.

A typical DCOP is formally represented as follows (Modi, Shen, Tambe, Yokoo, & Journal, 2005):

> *A DCOP consists of n variables $V=\{x_1,x_2,...,x_n\}$, each assigned to an agent, where the values of the variables are taken from finite, discrete domains $D_1,D_2,...,D_n$, respectively. Only the agent which is assigned a variable has control of its value and knowledge of its domain. The goal for agents is to choose values for variables such that a given global objective function is minimized. The objective function is described as the summation over a set of cost functions. A cost function for a pair of variables x_i and x_j is defined as $f_{ij}:D_i \times D_j \rightarrow N$. The objective is to find an assignment A^* of values to variables such that the aggregate cost F is minimized. The objective function F is defined as*
>
> $$F(A)=\sum_{x_i,x_j \in V} f_{ij}(d_i,d_j),\ \text{where}\ x_i \leftarrow d_i\ \text{and}\ x_j \leftarrow d_j\ \text{in}\ A.$$

Several DCOP solution searching algorithms have been proposed over the past years, such as Optimal Asynchronous Partial Overlap (OptAPO) (Mailler & Lesser, 2004), Distributed Pseudo-tree Optimization Procedure (DPOP) (Petcu & Faltings, 2005), Asynchronous Distributed Constraint OPTimization (ADOPT) (Modi et al., 2005), Asynchronous Branch-and-Bound ADOPT (BnB-ADOPT) (Yeoh, Felner, & Koenig, 2008) , BnB-ADOPT+(Gutierrez & Meseguer, 2010), and Concurrent Forward Bounding (ConcFB) (Netzer, Grubshtein, & Meisels, 2012). The above-mentioned algorithms only optimize one objective function.

Bowring et al. (2005) proposed a multi-criteria DCOP algorithm, called Multi-Criteria ADOPT and abbreviated as MCA, which is developed based on the ADOPT algorithm. This algorithm solves a multi-criteria DCOP by first transforming multi-criteria problem via virtual variables to single-criterion DCOP problems, revealing bounds on criteria to neighbors and then applying ADOPT to search for an optimal combination of parameter values. Bowring et al. (2005) defined the multi-criteria DCOP, which is a modified definition of DCOP, as follows. The multi-criteria DCOP defined by Bowring et al. (2005) is still a single objective optimization problem, though.

> *The objective of multi-criteria DCOP is to find an assignment A^* of values to variables such that F is minimized. The objective function F is defined as*
>
> $F(A) = \sum_{x_i, x_j \in V} f_{ij}(d_i, d_j)$, *where* $x_i \leftarrow d_i$ *and* $x_j \leftarrow d_j$ *in A. and*
>
> $\forall x_a \in V \;\; g_a^c(d_a, \{d_b \mid x_b \in neighbors(x_a)\}) \leq T_a^c, 1 \leq c \leq k$

Problems extended from the DCOP have been further drawn, including multi-objective DCOP (MO-DCOP) (Fave, Stranders, Rogers, & Jennings, 2011; Okimoto, Schwind, Clement, & Inoue, 2014), dynamic DCOP (DDCOP) (Yeoh, Varakantham, Sun, & Koenig, 2011), and dynamic MO-DCOP (DMO-DCOP)(Clement, Okimoto, Ribeiro, & Inoue, 2013).

The MO-DCOP is defined as a DCOP with multiple objective functions. Fave et al. (2011) proposed Bounded Multi-Objective Max-Sum algorithm (B-MOMS), and Okimoto et al. (2014) proposed Multi-Objective Lp-norm based Distributed Pseudo-tree Optimization Procedure (MO-DPOP$_{Lp}$) to solve the MO-DCOP.

The DDCOP is a sequence of the DCOPs with changes from one DCOP to the next one in the sequence. Yeoh et al. (2011) proposed the Incremental Search Algorithm for the DDCOP.

DMO-DCOP is a sequence of the MO-DCOPs. Okimoto, Clement, and Inoue (2013) proposed Aggregate Objective Function (AOF)-based algorithm, and Clement et al. (2013) proposed Dynamic Multi-Objective Branch and Bound (DMOBB) algorithm for the DMO-DCOP.

2.4 Agent-based Coordination Mechanisms

Coordination can be seen as the process of managing dependencies among activities. The procedure to coordinate activities is first identifying different kinds of dependencies between activities and then applying the coordination processes to manage them (Malone & Crowston, 1994). Weiss (1999) defined coordination as a property of a system of agents performing activities in a shared environment. Besides, Weiss (1999) shared his idea that the strategies for distributed planning and coordination can be: (1) post-planning coordination, (2) pre-planning coordination, (3) interleaved planning, coordination and execution, and (4) runtime plan coordination without communication. The degree of coordination is the extent to which they avoid extraneous activities by reducing resource contention, avoiding livelock, deadlock, and maintaining applicable safety conditions.

The nature of the multi-agent technology makes itself the best assistant in supporting coordination for mobile users. Researches or applications that apply the multi-agent technology to resolving conflict problems have sprung up in recent years. Sashima et al. (2004) proposed a conceptual framework, which is based on agent technologies, to coordinate human-centered services. Liu and Yao (2004) presented a methodology for developing Ubiquitous Agent Communities (UAC) and illustrated the coordinated services of a UAC with respect to an example of managing human daily tasks. Tafat, Courant, and Hirsbrunner (2005) proposed a generic coordination model (XCM), which is a context dependent ontology organized around a few abstract concepts (entity, environment, social law and port). Multi-agents in their study act as personal assistants that represent mobile users, and XCM is applied for agents to share their knowledge with others.

2.5 Scheduling Problems and Traveling Salesman Problems

The scheduling problems and traveling salesman problems are extensively applied to many practical areas. Gajski and Ramachandran (Gajski & Ramachandran, 1994) defined the scheduling problem as determining the sequence in which operations are executed to produce a control step schedule that specifies the operations executed in each control. Pinedo (1995) defined the scheduling as allocating limited resources to tasks over time. The traveling salesman problem is to find the cheapest way of visiting all of a given collection of cities. The scheduling problems and their problem-solving techniques are mapped and applied to the problems in computer systems, production planning, project management and public services. The traveling salesman problems are applied to the problems of circuit layout design, vehicle routing plan, and robot navigation.

Even though mobile users' activity scheduling for the on-site services may seem like the scheduling problems and the traveling salesman problems, it is quite different from the two. We survey the investigated scheduling problems and traveling salesman problems in this section and will make a comparison to show the differences later in Chapter 3.

Scheduling problems

The purpose of solving a scheduling problem is to find the optimum sequences for jobs to be operated in workshops under given constraints. T'Kindt and Billaut (2006) classified the scheduling problems into general typologies according to their characteristics as shown in Figure 2.1. The variant scheduling problems and their characteristics are presented in Table 2.1.

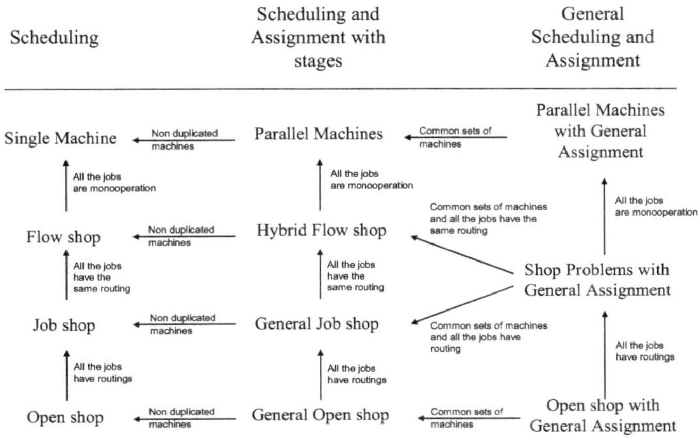

Figure 2-1 Typologies of scheduling problems (T'kindt & Billaut, 2006)

Table 2.1 Variant scheduling problems and their characteristics (T'Kindt & Billaut, 2002)

Types	Characteristics
Single machine	There is only one resource, and each job to perform is made up of only one operation.
Flow shop	The workshop is composed of *m* resources, and each job is made up of *m* operations. The jobs share the same routing.
Job shop	The workshop is composed of *m* resources. Each job is made up of *m* operations. Each job has its own routing in the workshop.
Open shop	The workshop is composed of *m* resources. Each job is made up of *m* operations. The routing of each job is not fixed.
Mixed shop	These problems are a combination of job shop and open shop problems.
Parallel machines	There is only one type of resources, which is gathered in one stage. Each job is made up of only one stage.
Hybrid flow shop	The workshop is composed of *k* stages, and each job is made up of *k*

Types	Characteristics
	operations. The jobs share the same routing through the stages.
General job shop	The workshop is composed of k stages. Each job visits the stages according to its own routing
General open shop	The workshop is composed of k stages. Each job visits the stages in a non-specified order.

The problem-solving approaches to scheduling problems can be classified into three categories: exact algorithm (Mingozzi, Maniezzo, Ricciardelli, & Bianco, 1998; Mokotoff, 2004), heuristic algorithm (Bankston & Harnett, 2000; Rajendran, 1995), and meta-heuristic algorithm (Feldmann & Biskup, 2003; Lee, Yu, & Xu, 2003; Liu, Ong, & Ng, 2005).

Traveling salesman problem

The purpose of solving a standard traveling salesman problem is to find the optimum route for a salesman who has to visit each of his interested or assigned locations exactly once. An extension of the traveling salesman problem, called multiple traveling salesmen problem, is practically applied to solving a wide variety of real-world problems.

The multiple traveling salesmen problem, abbreviated as mTSP, differing from the standard TSP, allows more than one salesmen to travel among locations. The purpose of solving the mTSP is to find routes for all the salesmen to minimize their total cost. Each salesman has to visit each of their interested or assigned locations exactly once.

The fundamental mTSP was first formulated by Bellmore and Hong in 1974. The fundamental mTSP was originally defined as follows:

In a multi salesmen problem, there are m salesmen available at a "base city" who are required to visit n "customer cities" and return to the base city. Here, each customer city must be visited exactly once by exactly one of the m salesmen and a cost is incurred if a salesman is actively used to visit customers. The problem is to determine how many of the m salesmen should be used and their routes to minimize the total distances traveled and costs incurred by all the salesmen.

Based on the fundamental mTSP, researches and practitioners from numerous fields have mapped a wide variety of real-world problems into mTSP and successfully solved their problems. Bektas in 2006 analyzed the mTSP cases and drew the characteristics of mTSP as listed in Table 2.2. The characteristics which help portray an mTSP are single/multiple depots, fixed/variable quantity of salesmen, fixed charges, time windows, and other special restrictions.

Table 2.2 Characteristics/Constraints of mTSP (Bektas, 2006)

Characteristics	**Descriptions**
Single vs. multiple depots	In the single depot case, all salesmen are required to start from a single location and return to the initial location once their travels are completed. In a multiple depots case, a certain number of salesmen are initially located at each location. After all salesmen complete their travels, the salesmen can either return to their initial location or any location with the restriction that the initial number of salesmen at each location must remain the same.
Fixed number of salesmen	If the number of salesmen is fixed, the quantity of salesman in the problem is previously determined. Otherwise, the quantity of salesman will be a bounded variable.
Fixed charges	If the quantity of salesman is a bounded variable and an extra fixed cost incurs whenever a salesman is employed, how to minimize the number of salesman should be considered while solving the problem.
Time windows	mTSP with time windows (mTSPTW) is a variation of standard mTSP, in which certain individuals need to be visited in specific time periods.
Other special restrictions	Other constraints, such as the number of individuals each salesman visits, the maximum or minimum distance a salesman travels or other special constraints.

Bektas (2006) also classified the cases of mTSP into seven major variations. These variations include (1) print press scheduling, (2) crew scheduling, (3) school bus routing problem, (4) interview scheduling, (5) mission planning, (6) hot rolling scheduling, and (7) design of global navigation satellite system surveying networks.

The problem-solving approaches to mTSP can be classified into three categories (Bektas, 2006): the exact algorithm (Ali & Kennington, 1986; Bellmore & Hong, 1974a; Gromicho, Paixão, & Branco, 1992; G Laporte & Nobert, 1980), heuristic algorithm (Fogel, 1990; Goldstein, 1990; Hsu, Tsai, & Chen, 1991; Modares, Somhom, & Enkawa, 1999; Potvin, Lapalme, & Rousseau, 1989; R. Russell, 1977; Sofge, Schultz, & DeJong, 2002; Somhom, Modares, & Enkawa, 1999; Song, Lee, & Lee, 2003; Tang, Liu, Rong, & Yang, 2000; Wacholder, Han, & Mann, 1989; Yu, Jinhai, Guochang, Rubo, & Haiyan, 2002; Zhang, Gruver, & Smith, 1999), and transformations to the TSP (Bellmore & Hong, 1974b; GuoXing, 1995; Hong & Padberg, 1977; Jonker & Volgenant, 1988; G. Laporte, Nobert, & Taillefer, 1988; M. Rao, 1980).

The characteristics of the MUCP are similar to those of the generalized open shop problem and the interview scheduling problem; however, they are different in many aspects. The generalized open shop scheduling problem arises in scheduling jobs in a workshop. In a generalized open shop problem, similar machines are collected into a stage to perform the same operations and the jobs, which visit the stages, can be scheduled in a non-specified order. Besides, for any job in this problem, each stage can be visited at most once.

The interview scheduling problem (Gilbert & Hofstra, 1992) arises in scheduling interviews between tour brokers and vendors, where each broker corresponds to a salesman and each vendor booth to a city. In the problem, each broker must visit a specified set of vendor booths, and at most one salesman per time period can visit one city.

A comparison will be made and differences will be drawn in Section 3.3. The scheduling problems and the traveling salesman problems are NP-complete problems.

The MUCP, despite possessing more complicated properties, can be reduced to those problems. The MUCP is also an NP-complete problem.

2.6 Computational Intelligence

Autonomic Computing

Autonomic computing is a promising concept which states that a system can manage itself autonomously according to its administrator's goals (Kephart & Chess, 2003). IBM defined the characteristics of an autonomic computing system with eight elements (Wolter, 2013) as below:

1. An autonomic computing system needs to "know itself", while its components must also possess a system identity.
2. An autonomic computing system must configure and reconfigure itself under varying conditions.
3. An autonomic computing system always looks for ways to optimize its workings.
4. An autonomic computing system must perform something akin to healing.
5. An autonomic computing system must be an expert in self-protection.
6. An autonomic computing system must know its environment and the context surrounding its activity, and act accordingly.
7. An autonomic computing system cannot exist in a hermetic environment.
8. An autonomic computing system will anticipate the optimized resources needed while keeping its complexity hidden.

With the autonomic computing ability, a system can maintain and adjust itself in face of the operating environment, monitor its own states and recover itself once error occurs. Ganek and Corbi (2003) shared the idea that autonomic computing is the next logical evolution to address the increasingly complex and distributed computing environments. Kephart and Chess (2003) said that the essence of autonomic computing is composed of at least one of the four functions, including self-configuration, self-optimization, self-healing and self-protection. Moreover, an autonomous system must be able to learn, evolve and self-adapt on feedback from the dynamic environment. Autonomic computing is realized in some pragmatically projects (Kaiser, Gross, Kc, Parekh, & Valetto, 2002; Matossian & Parashar, 2003).

Bantz et al. (2003) extended the concept of autonomic computing to personal computing and termed it autonomic personal computing. The architecture of autonomic personal computing is shown in Figure 2.2. Autonomic personal computing aims at simplifying and enhancing the end-user experience and helping the user anticipate his/her needs in the face of a complex, dynamic, and uncertain environment. Autonomic functions can be implemented by three different modes: locally, among members of a peer group, and using globally available network-resident resources. In the locally implemented mode, an autonomic personal system can make decisions by using knowledge that is stored or can obtained by itself. In the peer group mode, measurements and knowledge can be shared with its own group. In the network-based mode, the measurements and knowledge of any autonomic personal system are maintained and shared with all the others.

Autonomic personal computing has so far been mostly applied to software packages (Bantz et al., 2003), yet the idea is eligible for supporting mobile activities.

In the mobile environment, personal systems, the mobile devices, are distributed, heterogeneous and dynamically interconnected. Structure of the mobile environment changes moment by moment and the relations between personal systems are temporary and unpredictable. Under such conditions, real-time collaboration or coordination between systems is difficult to achieve. Autonomic computing, possessing the abilities of self-management, can offer great assistance to the mobile environment.

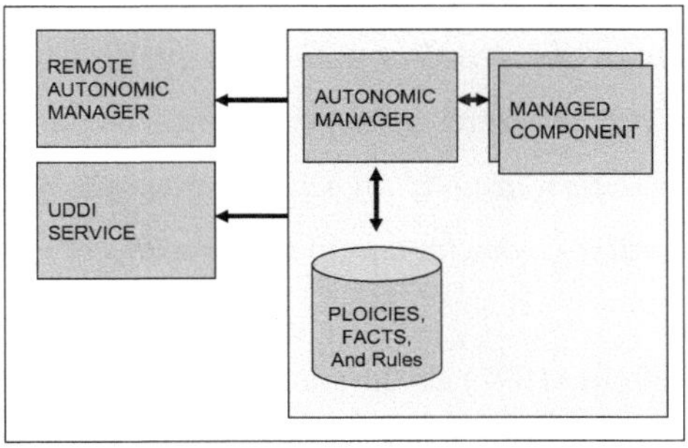

Figure 2-2 Architecture of autonomic personal computing (Bantz et al., 2003)

Humanoid intelligence

Robot Cog Project defined the humanoid intelligence as follows (http://www.ai.mit.edu/projects/humanoid-robotics-group/cog/overview.html):

"*Humanoid intelligence requires humanoid interactions with the world.*"

Ahmad (2004) indicated that the most important aspect of humans is their capability to learn and adapt. The two broad categories of human learning are interaction with the physical world and with fellow human beings. Ishiguro (2002) proposed a constructive approach to developing intelligent robots. The approach first gives a robot individual simple behaviors, and then the robot can develop its own complicated behaviors and intelligence through its interaction with the outside world. Ishiguro conducted some experiments and concluded that intelligence is a subjective phenomenon emerging from complicated interactions.

2.7 Forward Chaining Method

The forward chaining method is applied for mobile users to plan their personal activity schedules. We quote the description of forward chaining method stated in Luger and Stubblefield's book (1997):

The forward chaining method is a data-driven search technique, which begins with the given facts of the problem and a set of legal moves or rules for changing state. Search proceeds by applying rules to facts to produce new facts. The new facts in turn used by the rules to generate more new facts. The process continues until it generates a path that satisfies the goal condition.

Luger and Stubblefield (1997) further concluded that the data-driven search is appropriate to the problems in which: (1) all or most of the data are given in the initial problem statement; (2) there are a large number of potential goals, but there are only a few ways to use the facts and given information; (3) it is difficult to form a goal or hypothesis.

In the forward chaining method, the reception of new data can trigger new inferences, which makes the reasoning mechanism better suited to the dynamically changing context.

2.8 Pareto Improvement and Convergence to Global Optimality

Pareto improvement is an act to reallocate resources, and the reallocation makes at least one player better off without sacrificing anyone else. An allocation of resources is Pareto efficient or Pareto optimal when no further Pareto improvements can be made.

To avoid being trapped in local optimality, Sandholm (1996) defined an OCSM-contract type, denoting Original, Cluster, Swap and Multi-agent contract types, to achieve global optimal task allocation. Moreover, he proved that the global optimality could be reached by a finite number of contracts.

In the mobile environment, conflicts arise once service providers are fully booked up, and no additional reservation is acceptable. The conflicts are cooperatively resolved by exchanging the reservations of the conflict-related players. Before an exchange, the players must analyze the benefits and costs of making exchanges and then accordingly take actions. The players' benefits and costs are modeled based on the social exchange theory, and the reservation exchanges will be determined by the premise of Pareto improvement. Besides, although the OCSM-contract type is not designed for mobile users to plan their activity schedules, we apply the spirit of the OCSM to helping mobile users achieve joint optimality.

Chapter 3 MUCP Demonstration and Formulation

This chapter illustrates a simple example of the Mobile Users Coordination Problem (MUCP) to demonstrate our research. In this chapter, the MUCP is formulated into an MCDCOP. The required functionalities to solve it are accordingly derived.

We organize this chapter as follows. Section 3.1 cites a simplified MUCP to show the context of our research problem and the impact of context variation and exception on mobile users. Section 3.2 shows how mobile users plan and improve their personal activity schedules to reach joint optimality in the MUCP. Besides, this section demonstrates how mobile users' personal activity schedules are further improved to reach another joint optimality if context varies or exception happens. Section 3.3 compares the differences among the MUCP, the generalized open shop scheduling problem (GOSSP), the interview scheduling problem (ISP), and the DMO-DCOP. Plus, this section defines a general MUCP and formulates the MCDCOP for it. Section 3.4 characterizes the MCDCOP. Section 3.5 derives the requirements for solving the MCDCOP.

3.1 A Simplified Example of MUCP

Figure 3-1 presents a simplified example for the later demonstration of how independent mobile users plan and improve their activity schedules at a certain time point. The example is a general MUCP, which can be extended to the coordination of backpackers' itineraries, businessmen's visits to the booths of a business show, and tourists' use of facilities in a theme park.

In Figure 3-1, three service providers and six mobile users are involved. A time period with 36 time units is given to represent the business hours of the service providers. The time period is a temporal constraint to mobile users. If we map the MUCP into a traveling backpacker problem, the mobile users represent the backpackers and the service providers represent the tourist attractions. Backpackers are independent travelers who walk or use public transportation to visit tourist attractions for amusement and entertainment.

Three service providers, labeled A, B, and C, are located in the mobile environment to provide on-site services. The initial positions of A, B, and C, in the grid coordinates are (2, 6), (6, 5) and (3, 3), and the cycle times of the three service providers are set to be 7, 6 and 7 respectively. The capacities of the service providers are all set to be 1. Namely, during every cycle, each service provider is constrained to serve at most one mobile user. The number sets A[7,1] , B[6,1] and C[7,1] in the timetable charts in Figure 3-1 represent the cycle times and capacities of the service providers A, B, C respectively. For example, A[7,1] means that A's cycle time is 7 and A's capacity is 1. The symbols [A,1] , [A,2] ,..., represent the service durations of the 1st, 2nd, ..., cycles of A respectively.

The distances between A and B, B and C and C and A are respectively 5, 4 and 4 distance units. The time required for a mobile user to move from one service provider to another is assumed to be equal to their in-between distance, *e.g.*, moving from A to B or from B to A takes 5 time units.

Six mobile users, labeled from 1 to 6, are initially located in the grid coordinates as shown in Figure 3-1. They wander in the mobile environment to enjoy on-site services provided by A, B and C. Every mobile user carries a mobile device equipped with a GPS that helps them detect their instant position information and accordingly plan their activity schedule. A mobile user must previously book his/her desired services by the wireless network before enjoying it. In this example, every mobile user plans their personal schedule to maximize expected utility and minimize the cost while moving among the service providers. Before planning personal schedules, they must set an order of preference for desired services. The lower the preference order number, the higher the priority. Table 3.1 lists every mobile user's order of preference for service providers. In Table 3.1, the mobile user #1's preference order is $C \succ A \succ B$, which means that his/her preference order is C before A and A before B. To mobile user #1, his/her preference order number of C is 1, A 2 and B 3.

Table 3.1 Preference order of mobile users

Mobile user #	Preference order
1	$C \succ A \succ B$
2	$C \succ A \succ B$
3	$B \succ C \succ A$
4	$C \succ A \succ B$
5	$A \succ B \succ C$
6	$C \succ B$

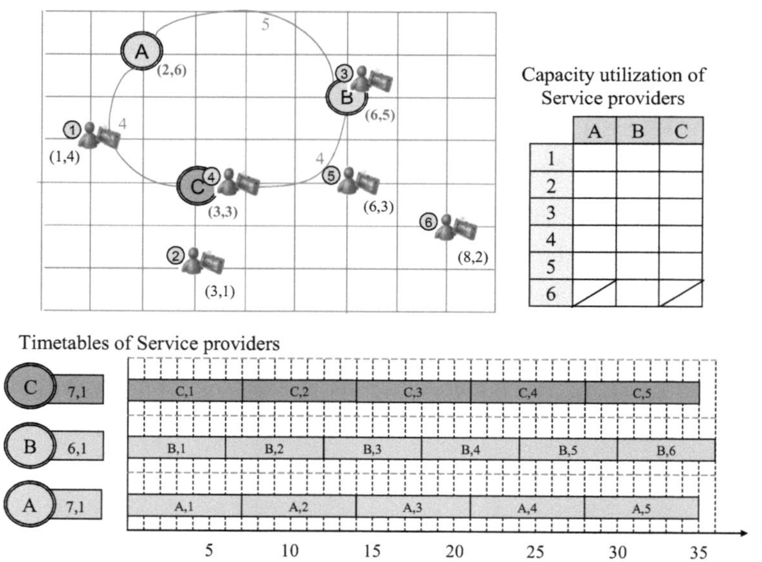

Figure 3-1 Example of planning activity schedules in the mobile environment

In the distributed mobile environment, every mobile user can have their own utility and cost structure to evaluate personal schedules. To make the demonstration simple, we assume that all mobile users use the same utility and expected cost functions to evaluate their schedules.

We adopt $u = \sum_{r=1}^{K} 1/\mathrm{p}(\tau_r)$ and $c = \mathrm{dist}(\Pi, \tau_1) + \sum_{r=1}^{K-1} \mathrm{dist}(\tau_r, \tau_{r+1})$ as the utility and cost functions respectively. The $\mathrm{p}(\tau_r)$ derives the preference order number of τ_r in a mobile user's schedule $\pi(\tau_1, \tau_2, .., \tau_r, .., \tau_K)$, with $\tau_1, \tau_2, .., \tau_r, .., \tau_K$ being desired activities. $\mathrm{dist}(\Pi, \tau_1) + \sum_{r=1}^{K-1} \mathrm{dist}(\tau_r, \tau_{r+1})$ sums up the total distance of the visiting route that starts from the mobile user's initial position Π, stops by the providers of $\tau_1, \tau_2 .., \tau_r, ..,$ and finally arrives at the provider of τ_K. In this example, a mobile user's preference is context-dependent, *e.g.*, weather conditions will affect a user's preference for the services.

Every service provider makes its reservation conditions, *e.g.* which cycle is available or is booked by whom, public on the Internet. In the mobile environment, server data are disseminated using either push-based or pull-based methods. In the push-based method, a service provider broadcasts data periodically to mobile users. In the pull-based method, a service provider responds to mobile users upon receiving their requests (Hall & Taubig, 2003). We assume that service providers open their reservation conditions using pull-based method.

Mobile users privately maintain their preference orders, estimate the satisfaction and cost upon the completion of their schedules, and accordingly plan their activity schedules. Shared Constraints, such as the capacities of service providers, and individual constraints, such as the temporal limit, put bounds on their schedules. Mobile users have access to the service providers' reservation conditions, whereas they have no access to the positions and preference orders of the other mobile users. Therefore, the mobile users' activity schedules are planned in the distributed environment.

To tackle the problem, we first enable every mobile user to optimally plan their personal schedule subject to the shared constraints and then to book the activities on the schedule. Once a mobile user has planned his/her own feasible schedule, and accordingly reserve his/her desired activities, we further enable him/her to improve his/her schedule. The improvement is achieved by having mobile users cooperatively coordinate their activities in the distributed environment.

3.2 Plan and Coordination of Activity Schedules

Section 3.2.1 illustrates how the mobile users individually plan their personal schedules, and Section 3.2.2 illustrates how the users cooperatively improve their schedules. Section 3.2.3 illustrates a context variance scenario to show the impacts on mobile users' decision makings and how mobile users respond to the impacts. Section 3.2.4 illustrates an exception scenario to show the impacts on users' schedules and how the exception is handled. Referring to the example and its scenarios, we formulate the MCDCOP for the MUCP and derive the requirements for tackling the problem.

What happens in the real environment is that mobile users simultaneously plan their schedules. However, in order to clearly describe how they optimize their schedules, we suppose that they plan and improve their personal schedules in turn.

3.2.1 Planning Schedules Individually

Mobile users, from #1 to #6, first plan their routes to visit the service providers according to their preference orders and the environmental situation as follows:

Mobile user #1: User #1's optimal visit route can be either C-A or vice versa, that is, either visiting C first and then A, or A before C. User #1 is not allowed to further visit B because of the temporal constraint. The C-A activity schedule, as shown in Figure 3-2-1, leads user #1's expected utility to be 1.5 (=1/1+1/2) and expected cost 7(=3+4).

Mobile user #2: User #2's visit route is C-A. If user #2 plans his/her schedule as Figure 3-2-2(a) shows, the capacity constraints of A and C in their second cycles will bring about conflicts. To resolve the conflicts, user #2 must re-plan his/her schedule. After re-planning, user #2's feasible schedule is shown in Figure 3-2-2(b).

Mobile user #3, #4, #5 and #6: User #3, #4, #5 and #6's optimal schedules subject to their immediate constraints are shown in Figure 3-2-3, 3-2-4, 3-2-5 and 3-2-6 respectively.

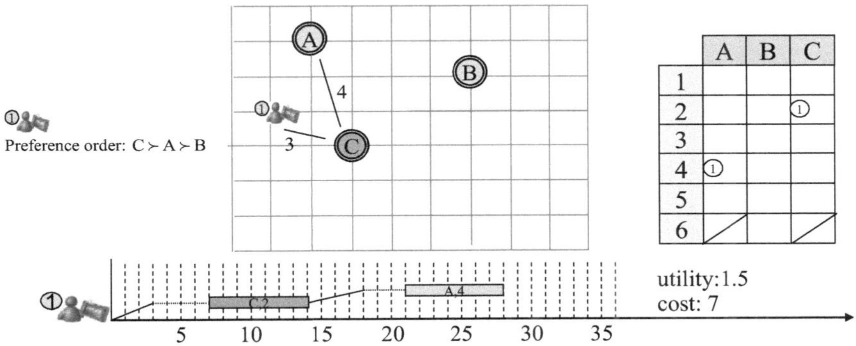

Figure 3-2-1 User #1's schedule

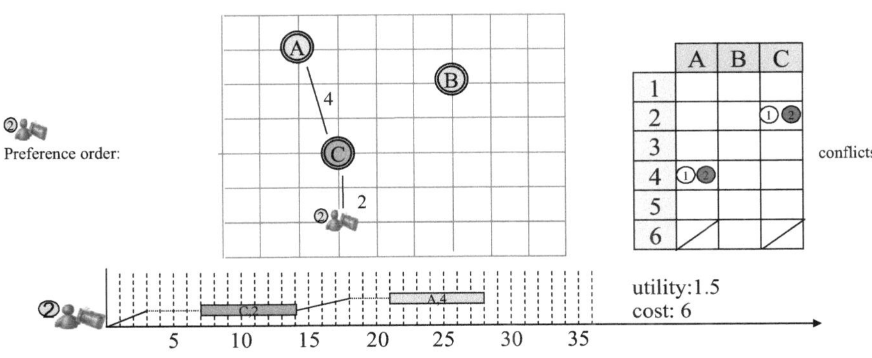

Figure 3-2-2(a) User #2's schedule (with conflicts)

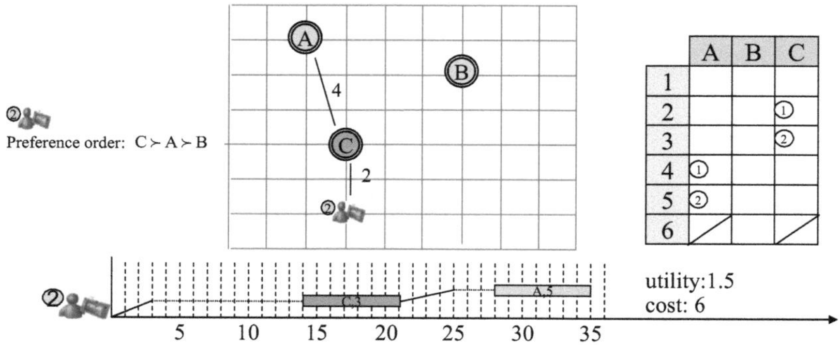

Figure 3-2-2(b) User #2's feasible schedule

Figure 3-2-2 User #2's schedule

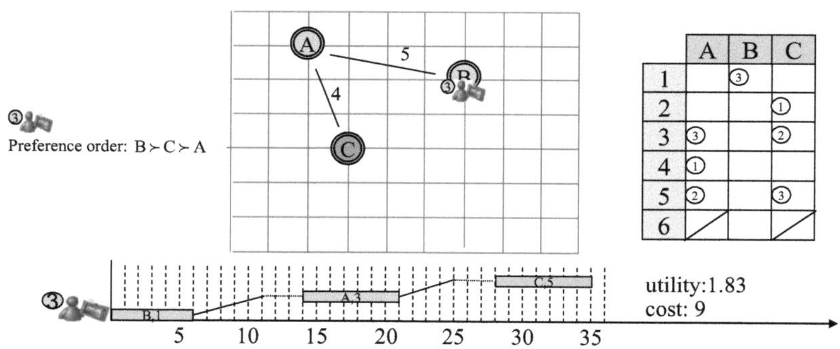

Figure 3-2-3 User #3's schedule

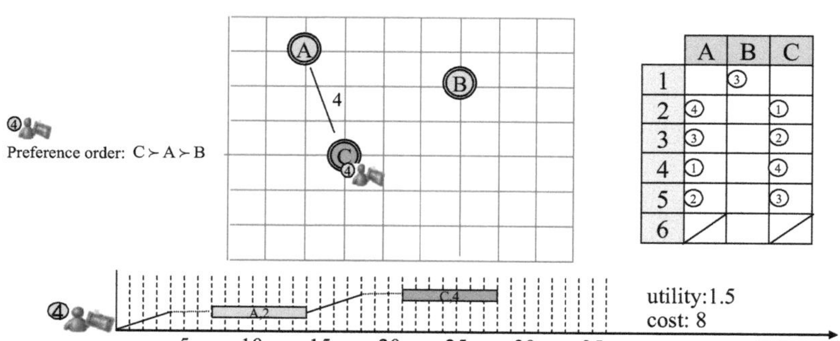

Figure 3-2-4 User #4's schedule

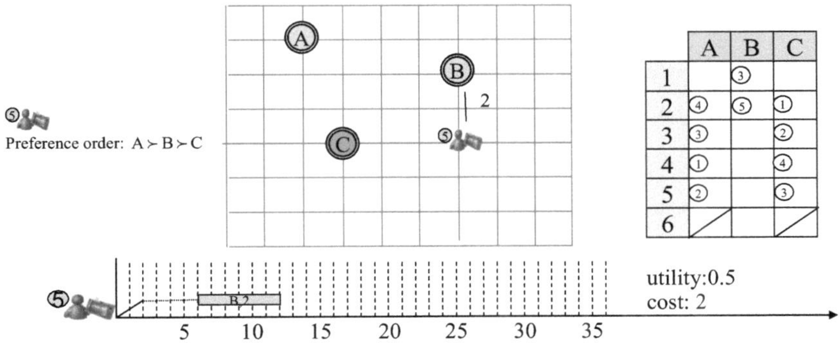

Figure 3-2-5 User #5's schedule

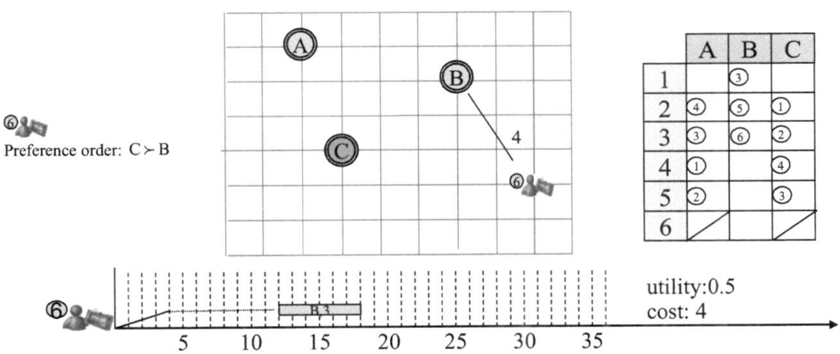

Figure 3-2-6 User #6's schedule

3.2.2 Improving Schedules Cooperatively

After having planned their schedules and reserved the corresponding activities, mobile users can further attempt to uplift their expected utilities or to lower their expected costs to improve their schedules.

In Figure 3-2-3, mobile user #3's expected utility and cost are respectively 1.83 and 9 subject to the providers' capacity constraints and the time limit. If we release the capacity constraints, user #3 can re-plan his/her schedule as shown in Figure 3-3-1. Figure 3-3-1 shows user #3's optimal schedule which reduces his/her cost from 9 to 8. To transform the original schedule in Figure 3-2-3 into the new one in Figure 3-3-1, user #3 must exchange reservations with the others. A comparison made between Figure 3-2-3 and Figure 3-3-1 shows that user #3 should exchange his/her 3rd cycle of A (simply called 3rd A) and the 5th C for the 5th A and the 3rd C. After asking service providers A and C about the reservation owners, user #3 then contacts user #2 to make a request for the exchanges. Receiving the request, user #2 assesses the effects of the exchanges. Figure 3-3-2 shows an assessment for user #2 in the case that the exchanges are accepted. In Figure 3-3-2, according to the "direct" assessment, user #2's utility remains the same but his/her cost increases from 6 to 10. User #2 thus rejects the request. User #3 is unable to improve his/her schedule.

However, if user #2 makes the assessment of the exchanges not so straightforward and tries to simulate what will happen after user #2 accepts user #3's request, a surprising result will come out. We assume that user #2 temporarily holds the reservations exchanged from user #3. With the reservations, user #2 re-plans his/her schedule as shown in Figure 3-3-3, his/her expected cost returns to the original value 6 and the utility still remains the same. To transform his/her schedule from Figure 3-3-2 to Figure 3-3-3, user #2 must do the same thing as user #3 does, namely, user #2 must exchange his/her 5th A and 3rd C for the 4th A and the 2nd C. After asking A and C about the reservation owners, user #2 then contacts user #1 to make a further request for reservation exchanges. Upon receiving the request, user #1 assesses the effects of the exchanges. Figure 3-3-4 shows the assessment, in which the expected utility and cost stay unchanged. User #1 thus can accept user #2's request, and then user #2 can accept user #3's request. User #3's schedule ends up with an improvement and users #1 and #2's schedules maintain the same quality.

Similarly, as shown in Figure 3-3-5, user #4 re-plans his/her schedule to exchange his/her 2nd A with user #1 for the 3rd A. After the exchange, user #4 can then reserve the additional activities, the 1st C and 6th B, without any conflict. A comparison of Figure 3-3-5 with Figure 3-2-4 shows that user #4's expected utility is uplifted from 0.83 to 1.83. User #4 significantly improves his/her schedule. As shown in Figure 3-3-6, user #5 reserves an additional activity, the 4th C. Consequently, his/her expected utility uplifts from 0.5 to 0.83.

The schedule improvement will be iteratively undertaken until no request can be accepted or no new reservation can be made. Finally, the involved users jointly obtain optimal schedules, and the service providers have their capacity utilization levels increased.

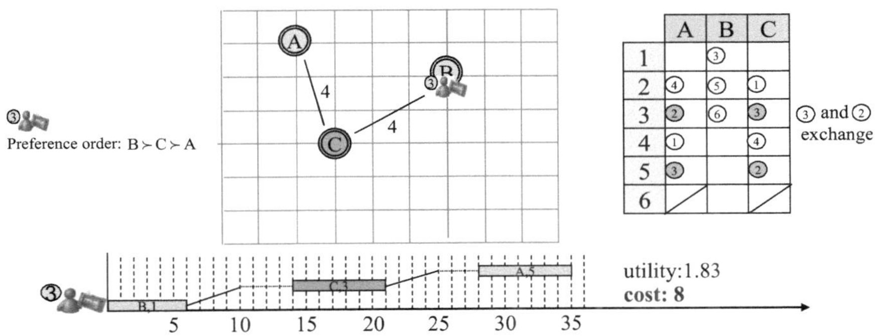

Figure 3-3-1 User #3's improved schedule and exchange scheme

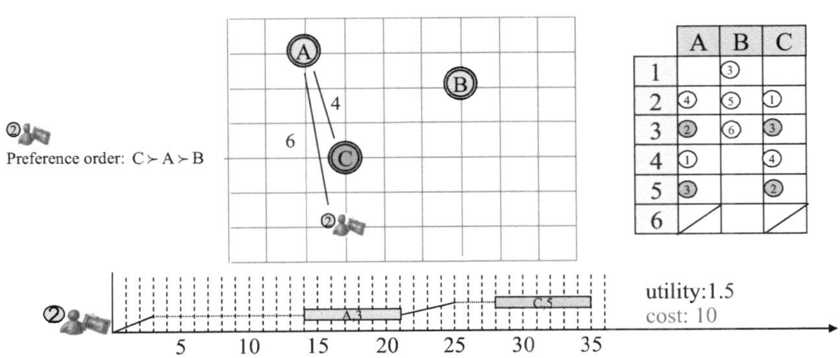

Figure 3-3-2 User #2's reservation exchange assessment

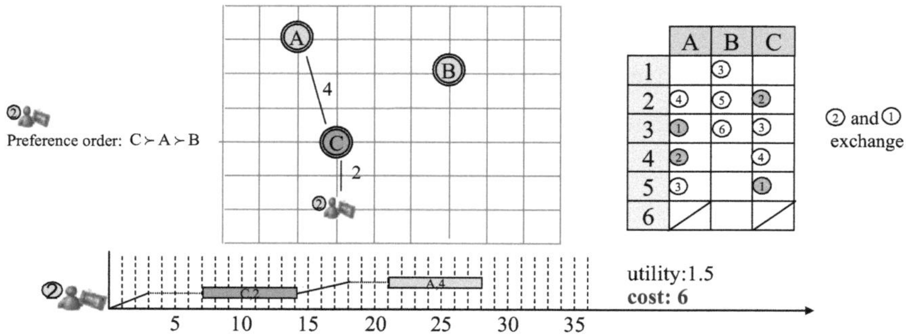

Figure 3-3-3 User #2's improved schedule and exchange scheme

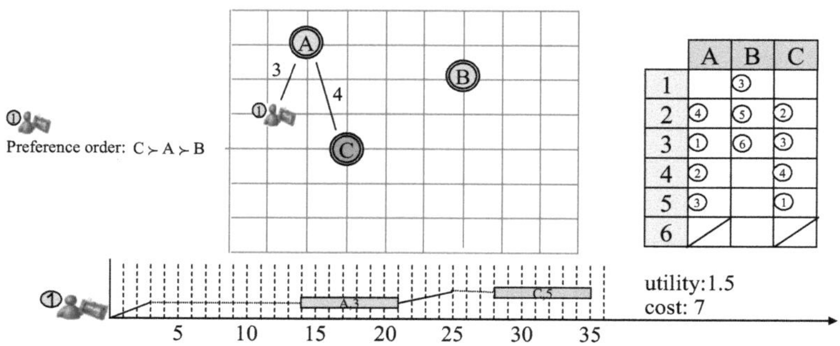

Figure 3-3-4 of User #1's new schedule after exchange

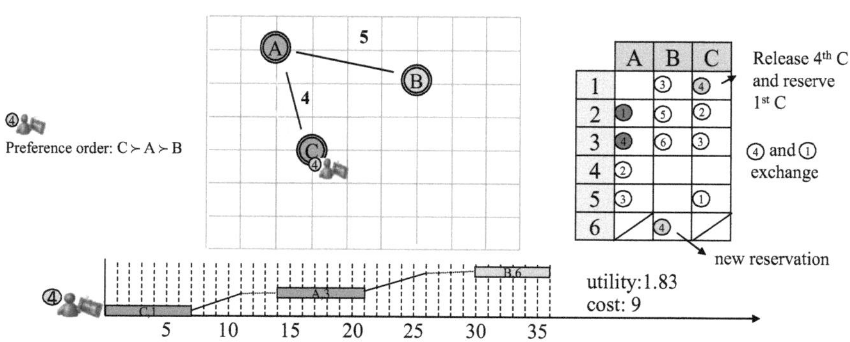

Figure 3-3-5 User #4's improved schedule and exchange scheme

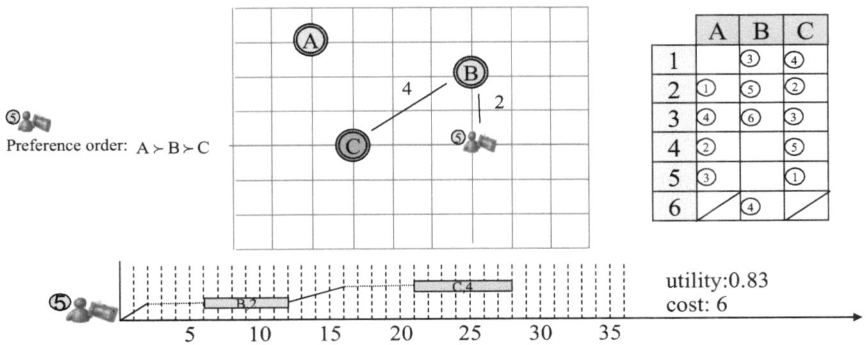

Figure 3-3-6 User #5's improved schedule

3.2.3 Improving Schedules for a Context Variation

To demonstrate how a context variation affects the mobile users' decision makings, we assume a scenario that takes place in the example in Figure 3.1 as follows:

After all users have jointly gotten their optimal activity schedules, the context suddenly varies and the variation affects user #2. User #2 adjusts his/her preference order from $C \succ A \succ B$ to $C \succ B \succ A$, which reduces his/her expected utility from 1.5 to 1.33 as shown in Figure 3-4-1. Therefore, user #2 may try to improve his/her schedule again. Figure 3-4-2 illustrates user #2's re-planned and improved schedule. In this figure, user #2 reserves a new activity, the 4th B, and releases one of his/her reservations, the 4th A. After the improvement, his/her expected utility returns to 1.5.

The release of 4th A brings a new opportunity for the other users to improve their schedules. For instance, in Figure 3-4-3, user #5 reserves the released 4th A, and releases his/her 4th C. Consequently, user #5 uplifts his/her expected utility from 0.83 to 1.5.

After user #5's release, another opportunity arises. In Figure 3-4-4, it is clear that user #6 can reserve the 4th C. However, user #6 cannot directly insert the 4th C into his/her schedule because after the completion of 3rd B, user #6 has insufficient time to arrive at C before the 4th C begins. User #6 must resolve the temporal conflict beforehand so as to improve his/her schedule. User #6 can exchange his/her 4th C for the 5th C of user #1 to get a new schedule as shown in Figure 3-4-5. As a result, user #6 uplifts his/her expected utility from 0.5 to 1.5. After the exchange, user #1's expected utility and cost stay unchanged as Figure 3-4-6 shows. In this way, the users can flexibly coordinate their activities and then maintain the joint optimality of their schedules despite the context variations.

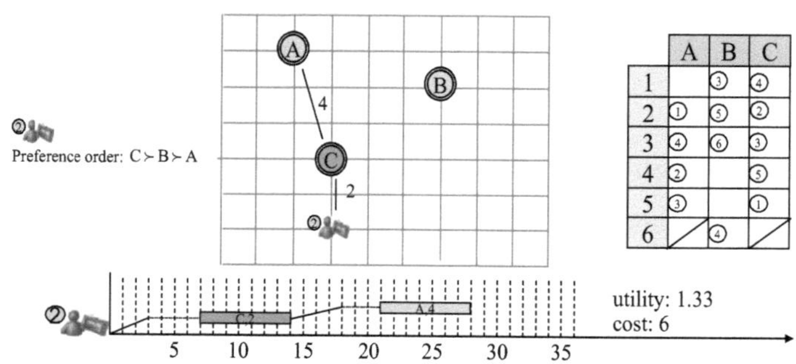

Figure 3-4-1 User #2's utility decrease after adjusting his/her preference order

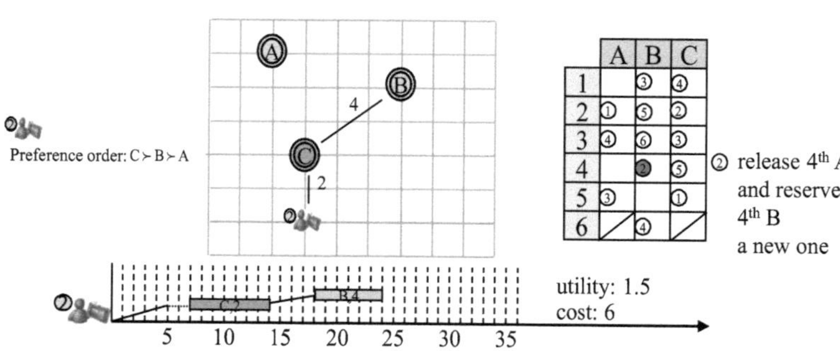

Figure 3-4-2 User #2's improved schedule

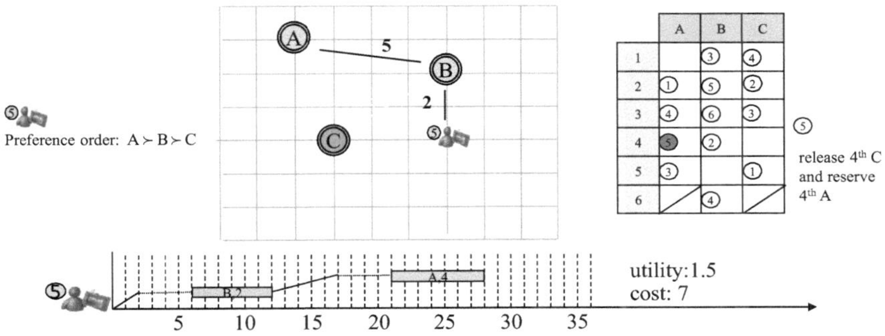

Figure 3-4-3 User #5's improved schedule

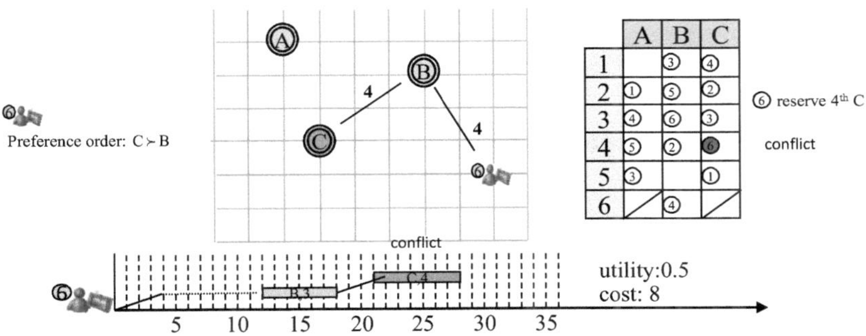

Figure 3-4-4 User #6's improved schedule and the activity conflict

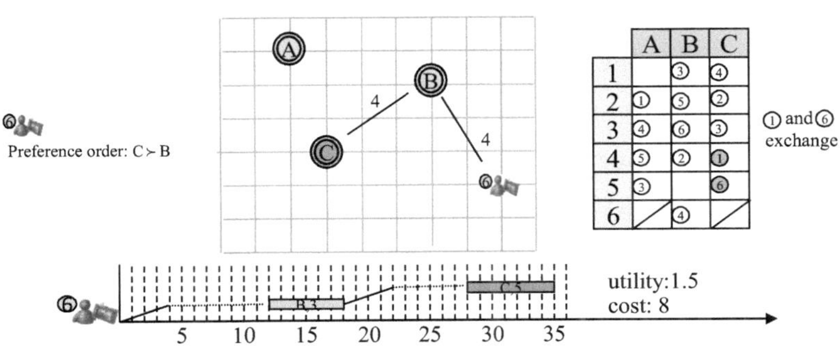

Figure 3-4-5 User #6's schedule and exchange scheme

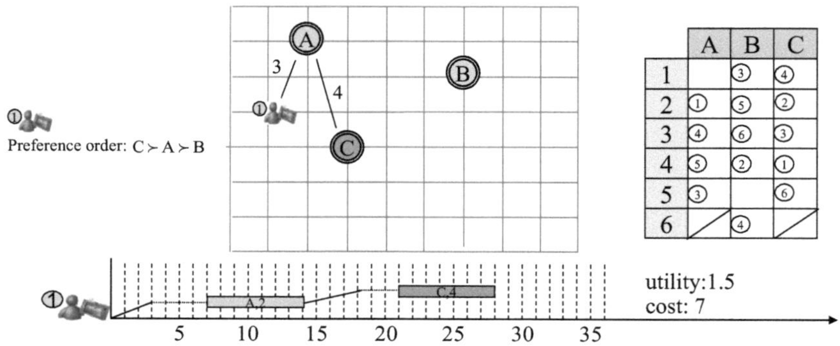

Figure 3-4-6 User #1's new schedule

3.2.4 Improving Schedules for an Exception

To demonstrate how an exception affects the mobile users, we assume a scenario in which an exception keeps a mobile user from successfully running his/her schedule and s/he wants to alter his/her schedule to reduce the impact. Let's go back to Section 3.2.2, in which all mobile users have jointly gotten their optimal schedules. The exception scenario is described as follows:

After user #5 has enjoyed the 2nd B and is ready to head for service provider C (at the end of time unit 12), a traffic problem happens, which makes user #5 unable to arrive at C before the 4th C begins. User #5 thus will alter his/her schedule by exchanging reservations with the others. Figure 3-5-1 shows user #5's re-planned schedule. In this schedule, s/he has to exchange his/her 4th C for the 5th C of user #1. Figure 3-5-2 shows user #1's new schedule after the exchange.

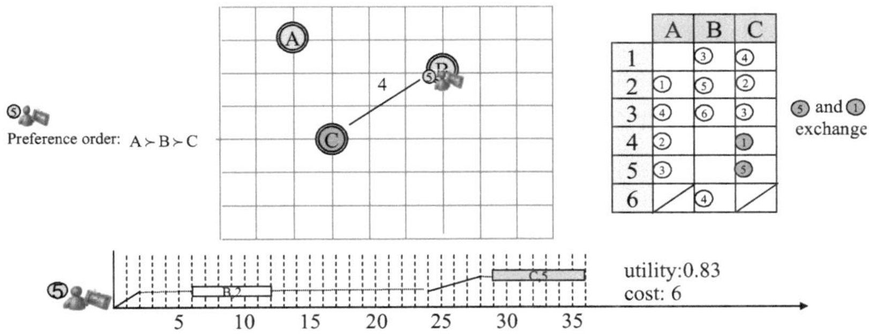

Figure 3-5-1 User #5's improved schedule and exchange scheme

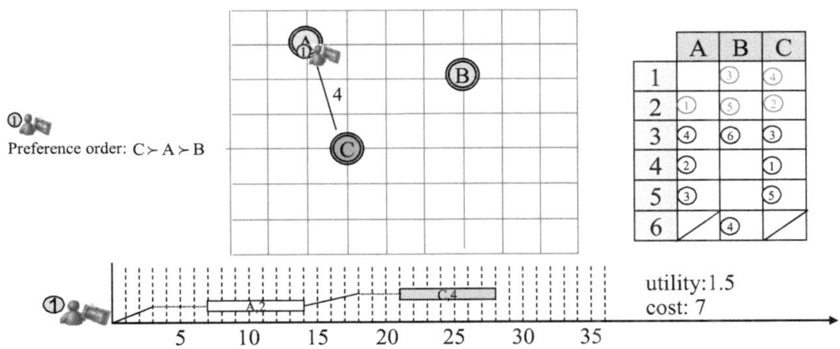

Figure 3-5-2 User #1 new schedule after the exchange

3.3 Formulating MUCP

The MUCP illustrated in Section 3.2 is a Multi-objective Context-dependent DCOP (MCDCOP). The MCDCOP is somewhat similar to the GOSSP and the ISP. A user in the MCDCOP corresponds to a job in the GOSSP and a broker in the ISP. A service provider in MCDCOP corresponds to a processor in the GOSSP and a vendor booth in the ISP. We make a comparison of their representative characteristics in Table 3-2 to highlight their differences and describe the differences as follows.

1. In the ISP, each broker must visit all the vendor booths just once. Similarly, in the GOSSP, each job must visit all the stages once. However, in the MUCP, each mobile user only visits his/her preferred service providers.
2. In the ISP and the GOSSP, all the brokers' or jobs' schedules are centrally planned to optimize their common objectives. In the MCDCOP, each mobile user proactively optimizes his/her personal objectives.
3. In the ISP and the GOSSP, all the variables and constraints are centrally controlled and managed. In the MCDCOP, all the variables and constraints are shared in distributed environment. That is, no one can control all of the variables and no one has complete information about the domains of the variables.
4. The ISP and the GOSSP do not take the impacts of context variation or exception into consideration, but the MCDCOP does.

Table 3.2 Characteristics comparison among MUCP, GOSSP and ISP

	Characteristics	**MCDCOP**	**GOSSP**	**ISP**
1	Places to visit	Not predetermined	Predetermined	Predetermined
2	Objectives	1.Distributed objectives 2.Planned by individuals	1. Global objective(s) 2. Planned centrally	1. Global objective(s) 2. Planned centrally
3	Variables and constraints	1.Shared in distributed environment	Controlled centrally	Controlled centrally
4	Context variation / Exception	Considered	Not considered	Not considered

Plus, the MCDCOP can be regarded as an extension of the DCOP. Table 3.3 presents the taxonomy of DCOPs according to their underlying characteristics. The MCDCOP is a dynamic multi-objective DCOP. Therefore, the MCDCOP and the DMO-DCOP (introduced in Section 2.3) are similar in problem characteristics; however, they are not alike in the following respects. (1) In the DMO-DCOP, all individuals have common objectives whereas in the MCDCOP, users are self-interested and pursue personal objectives. (2) In the DMO-DCOP, the number of individuals is fixed, whereas in the MCDCOP, the number of users is not fixed and users may enter or leave the mobile environment at any time. (3) In the DMO-DCOP, individuals form a fixed hierarchy, whereas in the MCDCOP, users are temporarily self-organized.

Table 3.3 Taxonomy of DCOPs

Problem category / Objective category		**Dynamic**	**Static**
Mono-objective		DDCOP	DCOP
Multi-objective	**Common-interests**	DMO-DCOP	MO-DCOP
	Self-interests	MCDCOP	Static MDCOP

Consequently, the comparison of characteristics aforementioned and shown in Tables 3.2 and 3.3 exposes that the problem-solving techniques for GOSSP, ISP or DMO-DCOP cannot be directly applied to MCDCOP. A new intelligent method is thus required for solving the conflicts that occur in the mobile environment.

We define the MCDCOP for the MUCP as follows. Accordingly, we formulate the MUCP.

An MCDCOP consists of n variables $V=\{x_1,x_2,...,x_n\}$, each assigned to an agent, with the values of variables taken from finite, discrete domains $D_1,D_2,...,D_n$ respectively. Only the agent which is assigned a variable has the control of its value and knowledge of its domain. Constraints are shared among the m agents. An agent i has its personal objective $f_i(X_i,C_t)$, where $X_i \subset V$ is the agent i's controlled variables, C_t is the time-variant context and i =1, 2,..., m. $X_i \cap X_{-i} = \phi$ where $i \neq -i$. The goals for agent i is to choose values for variables X_i such that its personal objective function always maintains optimization subject to the shared constraints g_j

and h_k and context variation C_t. g_j here is the equality constraint and h_k the inequality constraint. The MCDCOP is defined as follows:

$$\text{Minimize/Maximize } f_i(X_i, C_t),\ i=1,2,...,m$$

$$\text{Subject to}$$

$$g_j(x_1, x_2, ..., x_n) = 0$$

$$h_k(x_1, x_2, ..., x_n) \leq 0$$

The MCDCOP is a problem where more than one individual is involved in pursuing personal objectives and optimizing personal policies subject to shared constraints. Once an environmental context varies or any exception happens, some individuals are likely to adjust their policies. Briefly, this problem is a distributed constraint optimization problem; its objectives are distributed and multiple and are context-dependent and time-variant. We formulate the behaviors of the mobile users and the service providers in the MUCP as illustrated in Section 3.2 as follows.

***Service provider*:**

A set SP of M service providers, labeled $sp_1, sp_2, \ldots sp_i, \ldots, sp_M$, are located in a mobile environment to provide on-site services to mobile users in a given time period as shown in equation 3.1. The period contains T time units. The t in equation 3.2 denotes the tth time unit. Every service provider sp_i is characterized by a 4-tuple (S, δ, χ, η) as equation 3.3 shows. The four elements S, δ, χ and η respectively represent the features and conditions, service cycle time, capacity, and geographical location of a service provider. The first element S of sp_i in equation 3.4 is a set of paired variables $\{(s_1, \Phi_{1,t}), (s_2, \Phi_{2,t}), ..., (s_p, \Phi_{p,t}), ..., (s_L, \Phi_{L,t})\}$. The variable s_p is predetermined, which is the starting time of the pth service cycle. Equations 3.4 and 3.5 shows the relations between s_p and s_{p-1} as well as the constraint of s_L. In equations 3.4 and 3.6, the variable s_L is the last service cycle. The second variable $\Phi_{p,t}$, as shown in equations 3.4 and 3.7, is a set which exhibits the instant relations between the pth service cycle and every mobile user. $\Phi_{L,t}$ is the instant relations between the final service cycle and each mobile user. The $\Phi_{p,t}$ contains a list of variables $\{\varphi_{p,1}, \varphi_{p,2},..., \varphi_{p,j},..., \varphi_{p,N}\}$. As shown in equation 3.8, the value of the $\mathrm{sp}_i.\varphi_{p,j}$ shows whether or not the mobile user j makes reservation for the pth cycle of the service provider sp_i.

The other three elements δ, χ, η of sp_i are predetermined values as shown in equations 3.3, 3.9, 3.10 and 3.11. Element $\mathrm{sp}_i.\eta$ in equation 3.11 indicates the geographical location of sp_i, which denotes the x and y coordinates of sp_i.

Equation 3.12 shows the capacity constraints of the service providers. Every service cycle of every service provider can only accept limited reservations within its capacity. Equation 3.13 implies that no user can hold more than one reservation with a specific service provider sp_i .

$$\mathrm{SP} = \{\mathrm{sp}_i \mid 1 \le i \le M,\ i, M \in \mathrm{N}^+\} \quad (3.1)$$

$$t = \{t \mid 0 \le t \le T, t, T \in \mathrm{N}\} \quad (3.2)$$

$$\mathrm{sp}_i = \mathrm{sp}_i(\mathrm{S}, \delta, \chi, \eta) \quad (3.3)$$

$$\mathrm{sp}_i.\mathrm{S} = \{(\mathrm{s}_p, \Phi_{p,t}) \mid 1 \le p \le L,\ p, L \in \mathrm{N}^+\} \quad (3.4)$$

$$\text{if } p>1,\ \mathrm{sp}_i.\mathrm{s}_p - \mathrm{sp}_i.\mathrm{s}_{p-1} \ge \mathrm{sp}_i.\delta \quad (3.5)$$

$$\mathrm{sp}_i.\mathrm{s}_L + \mathrm{sp}_i.\delta \le T \quad (3.6)$$

$$\mathrm{sp}_i.\Phi_{p,t} = \{\varphi_{p,j} \mid 1 \le j \le N,\ j, N \in \mathrm{N}^+\} \quad (3.7)$$

$$\mathrm{sp}_i.\varphi_{p,j} = \begin{cases} 0 & \textit{if } \text{mobile user } j \text{ does not reserve the } p^{th} \text{ cycle of service } \mathrm{sp}_i \\ 1 & \textit{if } \text{mobile user } j \text{ reserves the } p^{th} \text{ cycle of service } \mathrm{sp}_i \end{cases} \quad (3.8)$$

$$\mathrm{sp}_i.\delta \in \mathrm{N}^+ \quad (3.9)$$

$$\mathrm{sp}_i.\chi \in \mathrm{N}^+ \quad (3.10)$$

$$\mathrm{sp}_i.\eta = (\mathrm{x}, \mathrm{y}),\ \mathrm{sp}_i.\mathrm{x}, \mathrm{sp}_i.\mathrm{y} \in \mathrm{R} \quad (3.11)$$

$$\forall i, p\ \sum_{j=1}^{N} \mathrm{sp}_i.\varphi_{p,j} \le \mathrm{sp}_i.\chi \quad (3.12)$$

$$\forall i, j\ \sum_{p=1}^{f_s} \mathrm{sp}_i.\varphi_{p,j} \le 1 \quad (3.13)$$

Mobile user:

A set MU of N mobile users, labeled mu_1, mu_2,…, mu_j,…, mu_N as shown in equation 3.14, wander in the mobile environment enjoying desired on-site services provided by the aforementioned service providers. Every mobile user mu_j is characterized by a 7-tuple $(\text{P}_t,\Omega_t,\Pi_t,\text{v},\pi_t^*,\pi_t^-,state_t)$ as equation 3.15 shows. The seven elements except v are context dependent and time variant. The seven elements $\text{P}_t,\Omega_t,\Pi_t,\text{v},\pi_t^*,\pi_t^-$ and $state_t$ respectively represent a mobile user's preferences, relations with service providers, position, average moving speed, optimal schedule, visited service providers and immediate state.

The 1st element P_t of mu_j in equations 3.15 and 3.16 is a set of paired variables $\{(\text{sp}_1,\text{p}_{1,t}),(\text{sp}_2,\text{p}_{2,t}),\ldots,(\text{sp}_i,\text{p}_{i,t}),\ldots,\ (\text{sp}_M,\text{p}_{M,t})\}$. The paired variable $(\text{sp}_i,\text{p}_{i,t})$ is used to record mobile user j's preference order number $\text{p}_{i,t}$, which corresponds to service provider sp_i at time t. The $(\text{sp}_M,\text{p}_{M,t})$ denotes the preference order number $\text{p}_{M,t}$, which corresponds to the last service provider sp_M. The $\text{p}_{i,t}$ is context-dependent, and the context may vary as time advances as shown in equation 3.17. The 2nd element Ω_t, in equations 3.15 and 3.18, is a set which exhibits the instant relations between the mobile user j and every service cycle of all the service providers. The Ω_t contains a list of variables $\{\omega_{1,1},\ \omega_{1,2},\ldots,\ \omega_{1,L},\ \omega_{2,1},\ \omega_{2,2},\ldots,\ \omega_{2,L},\ldots,\ \omega_{i,p},\ldots,\ \omega_{M,L}\}$. Equation 3.19 shows that the $\omega_{i,p}$ of mobile user j equals the $\varphi_{p,j}$ of service provider sp_i. The Π_t in equation 3.20 denotes the instant position of mobile user j at time t. The 4th element v in equation 3.15 is the average moving speed of mobile user mu_j. $\text{mu}_j.state_t$ in equation 3.21 denotes the immediate state of mobile user mu_j. A mobile user in the mobile environment will be in one of the five states as shown in equation 3.21. The state is used to regulate a mobile user's behaviors, which will be explained later in Section 5.2.

$$\text{MU}=\{\text{mu}_j \mid 1\le j\le N,\quad j,N\in \text{N}^+\} \quad (3.14)$$

$$\text{mu}_j=\text{mu}_j(\text{P}_t,\Omega_t,\Pi_t,\text{v},\pi_t^*,\pi_t^-,state_t) \quad (3.15)$$

$$\text{mu}_j.\text{P}_t = \{(\text{sp}_i, \text{p}_{i,t}) \mid 1 \le i \le M, \text{p}_{i,t} \in \text{N}^+\} \quad (3.16)$$

$$mu_j.\text{p}_{i,t} = mu_j.\text{p}(\text{sp}_i, context_t) \quad (3.17)$$

$$\text{mu}_j.\Omega_t = \{\omega_{i,p} \mid 1 \le i \le M, 1 \le p \le L\} \quad (3.18)$$

$$\text{mu}_j.\omega_{i,p} = \text{sp}_i.\varphi_{p,j} \quad (3.19)$$

$$\text{mu}_j.\Pi_t = (x_t, y_t),\ \ x_t, y_t \in \text{R} \quad (3.20)$$

$$\text{mu}_j.state_t \in \{\text{'Fresh', 'Live', 'Locked', 'Solitary', 'Off-line'}\} \quad (3.21)$$

A mobile user thus will plan his/her schedule to enjoy desired activities as shown in equations 3.22 to 3.27. The 5th element π_t^* of mu$_j$ in equation 3.22 shows mobile user *j*'s optimal policy at *t*, which is a set of paired service providers. Each pair $(\tau_{r,m}, \tau_{r+1,n})$ represents the optimal order of how mu$_j$ visits the service providers and which service cycle s/he plans to enjoy. For example, $(\tau_{r,m}, \tau_{r+1,n})$ means that the user will enjoy the mth service cycle of the service provider τ_r (τ_r can be any service provider sp) first and then enjoy the nth service cycle of the service provider τ_{r+1}. Several pairs are linked together to form mu$_j$'s optimal route. The 6th element π_t^- in equation 3.23 records visited service providers before t , which will not be visited again in equation 3.22. Namely, no service provider can be visited more than once.

A mobile user's objective is to maximize his/her expected satisfaction es_t at *t*, as shown in equation 3.23. The expected satisfaction is a function of expected utility and cost at time *t*, as shown in equation 3.25. The constraints to user mu$_j$ are shown in equations 3.12, 3.25, 3.26 and 3.27. Equation 3.12 is the capacity constraint, whereas equations 3.26, 3.27 and 3.28 are temporal constraints. Equation 3.25 constrains user mu$_j$'s schedule to make his/her desired activities within the given time period *T*. Equation 3.26 also constrains mu$_j$'s schedule to assert that s/he must be able to arrive at the first service provider's location before enjoying the service. In equation 3.26, the dist is a function to compute the distance between mu$_j$'s initial postion Π and the location of first desired service provider τ_1.

Equation 3.27 relates every activity and its next activity to assert that mu_j must be able to arrive at the next service provider's location before enjoying the on-site service.

Plan

$$\mathrm{mu}_j.\pi_t^* = \{(\tau_{r,m}, \tau_{r+1,n}) \mid \tau_r, \tau_{r+1} \in \mathrm{SP} - \pi_t^-, 1 \le r \le K-1, \quad m,n,r,K \in \mathrm{N}^+\} \qquad (3.22)$$

$$\mathrm{mu}_j.\pi_t^- = \{\hat{\tau}_q \mid \hat{\tau}_q \in \mathrm{SP}, \hat{\tau}_q \text{ is visited}, q \in \mathrm{N}^+\} \qquad (3.23)$$

Maximize

$$\mathrm{mu}_{j.}es_t = f(\mathrm{mu}_{j.}eu_t, \mathrm{mu}_{j.}ec_t) \qquad (3.24)$$

Subject to

$$\mathrm{t} + \sum_{r=1}^{K} \mathrm{mu}_j.\tau_r.\delta + \sum_{\mathrm{r}=1}^{K-1} \mathrm{dist}(\tau_r.\eta, \tau_{r+1}.\eta) / \mathrm{mu}_j.\mathrm{v} \le T, \quad \mathrm{mu}_j.\mathrm{v} \in \mathrm{N}^+ \qquad (3.25)$$

$$\mathrm{dist}(\mathrm{mu}_j.\Pi_t, \tau_1.\eta) / \mathrm{mu}_j.\mathrm{v} \le \tau_\mathrm{r}.\mathrm{s}_m \qquad (3.26)$$

$$\forall r \ \ \tau_\mathrm{r}.\mathrm{s}_m + \tau_\mathrm{r}.\delta + \mathrm{dist}(\tau_r.\eta, \tau_{r+1}.\eta) / \mathrm{v} \le \tau_{\mathrm{r}+1}.\mathrm{s}_n \qquad (3.27)$$

3.4 Characterizing MCDCOP and MUCP

Referring to the example demonstrated in Section 3.1, 3.2 and the problem formulation in Section 3.3, we abstractly characterize the MCDCOP as follows, which will be considered to develop valid techniques for tackling the problem in Sections 4 and 5.

1. The MCDCOP is a distributed optimization problem. More than one individual is involved in the problem. In the mobile environment, an individual owns only incomplete information and is incapable to control and manage all of the variables.
2. The MCDCOP is a multi-objective optimization problem. In this problem, every individual pursues his/her personal objective subject to the shared constraints. The objective and constraints are parameterized and are composed of some variables.

3. The MCDCOP is a context-dependent optimization problem and the context may vary as time advances. An individual's objectives are very likely to be affected once the context varies.
4. To solve an MCDCOP is to find a joint optimal solution, which is a combination of all individuals' policies.
5. Constraints, which put bounds on individuals' policies in the MCDCOP, can be categorized into two independent types, including the internal and external constraints. The internal constraints, such as the temporal constraint, are those that individuals face personally. The external constraints, such as the capacity constraints, are those that individuals face commonly and are shared among individuals.
6. The optimal policy combination is under the condition that there exists no other combination that makes every individual at least as well off and at least one individual strictly better off.

We further derive additional and solid characteristics for the MUCP based on the MCDCOP as follows.

1. A user's objective is to plan his/her policy to maximize his/her expected satisfaction. The policy is an activity schedule for the user to enjoy his/her desired activities. Therefore, in the MUCP, the combination of users' activity schedules is their joint policies.
2. The mobile environment is not in a static condition. Exceptions are likely to happen. If a user runs into an exception, s/he tends to adjust his/her schedule to reduce the impacts of the exception.
3. Once a context variation or an exception affects a user's preferences on the activities, the schedule combination to the problem needs to be improved to maintain optimality. The improvement is not carried out by resetting and re-planning all mobile users' schedules, instead, it is by the coordination and the adjustment. Resetting and re-planning is not a fair way for most mobile users since the context variation or exception does not pervasively affect all

users. Adjustment thus is appropriate. The adjustment of schedule combination is made by the related mobile users to exchange their reservations.

4. The temporal and capacity constraints put limits on every mobile user's schedule. The mobile users' schedules must be feasible and with no conflicts. The temporal constraints restrict mobile users to planning their schedules and arranging their desired activities into a finite time period. Moreover, in the mobile users' schedules, the commute time must be sufficient for the users to move from one service provider to the next. The capacity constraint is that the service providers can only accommodate limited users in their every service cycle. Besides, a mobile user cannot enjoy the same service more than once.
5. The incomplete information is that the users will not reveal their private information, such as their positions or preferences, to others. The information that the users can gather is from the service providers. The service providers open the information of their detailed reservation conditions, including who (represented by virtual figures, *e.g.*, agents) owns which service cycles, to all users.

3.5 Requirements for Solving MCDCOP

After analyzing the characteristics of the MUCP and MCDCOP, we derive the required functionalities for the developing problem-solving techniques as follows:

1. The problem-solving techniques must be able to not only support mobile communication for users to interact with the others but also to support real-time and online coordination.
2. The problem-solving techniques must function to support mobile users in planning, obtaining and then improving their optimal activity schedules subject to the shared constraints with incomplete information. A new mobile user, once entering the mobile environment, can employ the techniques to plan and obtain his/her personal schedule with respect to his/her immediate situations and the shared constraints. After that, the user can further employ

the techniques to cooperatively improve his/her schedule with the others. Moreover, if a context variation or an exception impacts a mobile user's objective or schedule, s/he can employ these techniques to improve his/her schedule.

3. A decentralized coordination mechanism and a reservation exchange protocol are required to support the mobile users in cooperatively improving their personal schedules. The decentralized coordination mechanism defines how mobile users can self-organize loosely-coupled coordination networks. The reservation exchange protocol designs the language standards and defines the rules for mobile users to exchange their reservations.

Grounded on the derived functionalities, a multi-agent framework, SPA, and a two stage optimization technique, 2S-DORA, are proposed for solving the MCDCOP. We respectively elaborate the SPA in Chapter 4 and the 2S-DORA in Chapter 5.

Chapter 4 SPA: Integrated Multi-agent Systems

This chapter introduces the characteristics of multi-agents, the integrated multi-agent systems SPA (Lin & Lin, 2006) and the multi-agent platforms applied to implement SPA. We organize this chapter as follows. Section 4.1 characterizes the simulated agents and the physical agents. Section 4.2 elaborates the framework of SPA. Section 4.3 presents our employment of the multi-agent systems and the implementation of SPA.

4.1 Characteristics of Simulated and Physical Agents

The multi-agent technologies are broadly applied to many fields. Among all of the applications, there are basically two types of agent designs: simulated and physical agents. Simulated agents are an individual based modeling tool, which allows researchers to use the bottom-up approach to decompose a problem into many sub-problems. Researchers can observe the autonomous interactions of the agents in the sub-problems, and then observe the collective effects of the agents' interactions. The decomposition can simplify a complex problem which facilitates researchers' examination of their problems in both micro- and macro-views.

Physical agents are the agents that can interact with the real-world environment via the network. Physical agents can maintain their own state, sense the outside world variations, exchange messages with other related physical agents and perform a series of tasks to achieve their given goals.

We take advantage of both simulated and physical agents to facilitate mobile users' coordination of their activities in the mobile environment. Simulated agents maintain a true belief mechanism about users' outside world. They capture the structure of the other users and their corresponding behavioral logics. The simulated agents can simulate and analyze the interactions of the related users and support decision makings to enable mobile users to respond to the dynamic environmental changes. Physical agents on behalf of a mobile user can communicate, coordinate, and collaborate with users' related physical agents that represent other mobile users.

4.2 Framework of SPA

The integrated multi-agent systems, called SPA by extracting initials of the Simulated and Physical Agents, is shown in Figure 4-1. In Figure 4-1, physical agents represented as star-shaped entities, interact with the physical agents of other users based on the decision alternatives suggested by simulated agents. The SPA, utilizing the corresponding capabilities of simulated and physical agents with built-in intelligence, is assembled from four major modules: analytic and reasoning module, sensory module, social module and self-management module. These four modules are elucidated as follows.

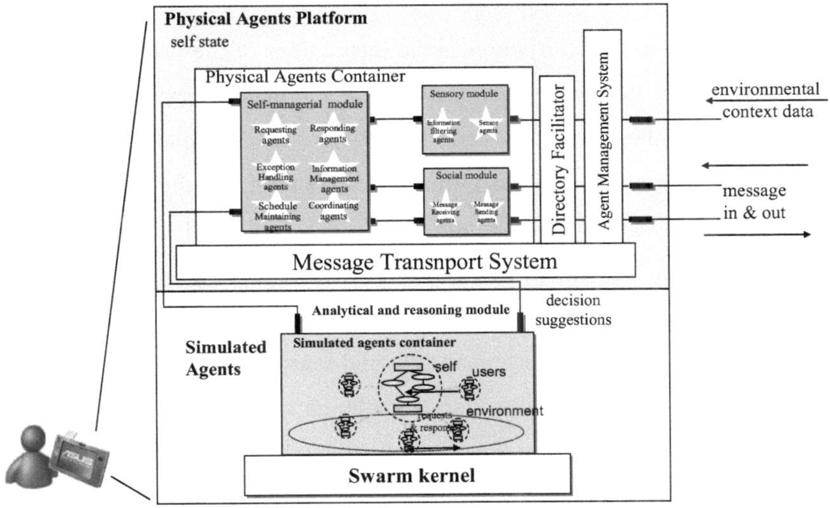

Figure 4-1 Framework of SPA

Analytic and reasoning module

The analytic and reasoning module is made up of simulated agents. The module is composed of the agent's belief, a scenario simulation facility and analyzing and reasoning facility. Simulated agents in each agent system simulate the what-if scenarios of the mobile environment, analyzing the simulated results, reasoning the to-be-solved problems and proposing suggestions. Physical agents thereafter will act on the suggestions offered by the simulated agents.

An agent's belief is a self-developed cognitive structure which is the perception of the outside world by an agent itself. The belief of an agent has a deep influence on its behaviors and decision-makings. The belief system of a user maintains its view on the status of the mobile environment and the related users. The belief system gathers information via the sensory and social modules of physical agents, where information could be the structure of the interactive environment, the user's personal state, the environmental context and the message exchanged with the other mobile users. The belief system helps the simulated agents analyze their gathered information and reason out their problems. Users can accordingly make decisions and then take actions.

A scenario simulation facility models the interactions of the users in the mobile environment based on the agent's belief. In Figure 4-1, agents located in the biggest circle and placed in the center represent the activity schedule planned by the user himself/herself, and agents in the other smaller circles represent the schedules of the other related users. The agents can represent a user's desired activities and the corresponding service providers. The data needed for these simulated agents to simulate and analyze schedules can be input from the agent's belief. The scenario simulation facility is invoked by the analyzing and reasoning facility. The analyzing and reasoning facility will give the scenario simulation facility a preset scenario. The scenario will then be simulated and the results finally will be returned back.

The analyzing and reasoning facility can be invoked once a new schedule is to be planned, the context variation of the environment is detected, or any exception happens. As shown in Figure 4-1, the simulated mobile environment will always maintain equilibrium by the analyzing and reasoning facility no matter what happens. The equilibrium will support decision makings for mobile users.

The mobile environment is complicated and highly dynamic. Besides, to protect individual privacy, all users won't share their complete information, such as location and preferences. That is, all mobile users are constrained by the bounded rationality. Moreover, based on the given social theories, such as social exchange theory, the analytic and reasoning module can be used for analyzing alternative policies in planning activity schedules. In this manner, the collection of simulated agents acts as a decision support system to facilitate the decision making. The alternatives suggested by the simulated, analyzed and reasoned results contribute to corresponding physical agents in making decisions.

Sensory module

The sensory module is developed to periodically detect the dynamics of the mobile environment and extract important contextual information from the mobile environment. The sensory module contains two sorts of physical agents, the sensor, and information filtering agents. The sensor agents serve as detectors to detect the context via context sensors or act as receivers to receive information from contextual information providers. The information filtering agents serve as filters to filter out valueless information. The collected contextual information will be transferred to the self-management module and then be used to update the belief of analytic module.

Social module

The social module gives SPA the social behaviors that enable a mobile user to remotely interact with other users. The social module contains two sorts of physical agents: the message receiving and sending agents, and a predefined communication ontology. Based on the ontology, mobile users with social abilities can communicate with others, organize temporary coordination networks, exchange their information, adjust themselves and coordinate with other mobile users to reach conflict free activity schedules based on the knowledge and suggestions provided by simulated agents.

Self-management module

The self-management module maintains a user's all exchanged information, his/her context-dependent objectives, and his/her activity schedules. Moreover, the module handles the exceptions. The self-management module contains six sorts of physical agents: requesting, responding, exception handling, information management, objective and schedule maintaining, and coordinating agents.

The requesting agents are designated to request necessary information for simulated agents, and responding agents on the other are to answer the coming requests. During the coordination process, the responding information from the other physical agents can feed to the simulated agents to conduct a new cycle of simulation and analysis, and to propose alternative suggestions, which will be used to resume the coordination process by physical agents.

The exception handling agents serve as a facilitator to deal with the happening of some condition that the normal or predetermined plans are changed. Once perceiving an exception, the exception handling agents will invoke the analyzing and reasoning agents and the schedule maintaining agents to execute new simulations to re-plan new workable schedules.

The information management agents serve as an administrator to store and control the sharing of all information. The objective and schedule maintaining agents are designated to work with the analytic and reasoning module to plan and maintain a user's schedule. Once a conflict happens, objective and schedule maintaining agents will first invoke the analytic and reasoning module to execute simulations and then invoke the coordinating agents to start the coordination process.

The coordinating agents are designated to organize coordination networks while coordination is required. The coordinating agents work with the analytic module and the social module to resolve the conflicts that occur in the mobile environment. Since in the mobile environment, the structure of the coordination network is highly dynamic and the relations between mobile users are short, coordinating agents must be able to form a coordination network quickly. Figure 4-2 illustrates the temporarily organized coordination network in which related SPAs interact with each other to coordinate the mobile activities of corresponding mobile users. The interaction between physical agents and simulated agents facilitates the planning and improving of the activity schedules.

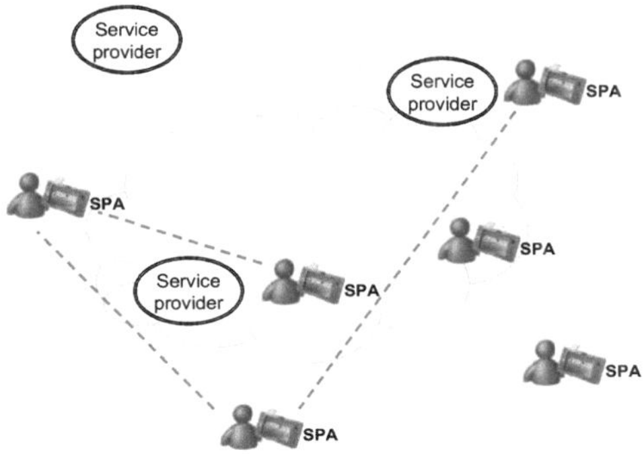

Figure 4-2 Interaction of SPAs for coordinating mobile activities

4.3 Employment of Multi-agent Platforms

There are many agent platforms available for researchers and practitioners to rapidly develop their own multi-agent systems. Most of these platforms are cost-free and ease of use. RePast, Swarm, Quicksilver, and VSEit are well-known simulated agent platforms (Weidmann & Girardin, 2005). JADE, Zeus, FIPA-OS are popular physical agent platforms. Every platform has its own features and can be applied to specific domains. We employ Swarm as the simulated agent platform, and JADE the physical agent platform. Both of these two platforms are java-based and thus can be integrated seamlessly to cooperate with each other. SPA thus can make full use of the simulated and physical agents. These two platforms are introduced as follows.

Swarm simulated agent system

Swarm is a multi-agent simulation platform initiated by Santa Fe Institute (Minar, Burkhart, Langton, & Askenazi, 1996), which became the Swarm Development Group later (see http://www.swarm.org). Swarm is composed of a set of object libraries, which allow users to construct objects to represent agents and their actions. Swarm is a general-purpose package for simulating a concurrent and distributed artificial world. The core of Swarm is an object-oriented framework for defining an agent's behaviors and the interaction between agents during simulation. In the Swarm, an agent consists of the following components: (1) a data structure that contains an agent's internal state variables, (2) a step function that initializes an active agent's action, and (3) action functions that are triggered by the message sent from its environments (i.e., from other agents or simulation control objects).

Swarm uses an individual-based modeling approach, which allows each agent to have its own set of internal state variables. Individual agents have their local views of the world, and the combination of the individual behaviors shapes up the collective behaviors of the whole group. In the Swarm system, an agent can itself be a swarm of agents. This hierarchical inheritance can be a depth of several layers, and this property is called the nested inherent hierarchy as shown in Figure 4-3. A swarm can be represented by a set of agents coordinating at various levels in or between mobile users. Moreover, Swarm is not just a collection of objects but also a schedule. The recursive management of time supports an entire spectrum of synchrony management ranging from the strict, top-down and lock-step synchrony managed by a single sequential executor to the loose asynchrony with effective parallelism. Swarm simulation platform has been applied to many domains, such as economics, finance, business, etc. (Luna & Stefansson, 2000).

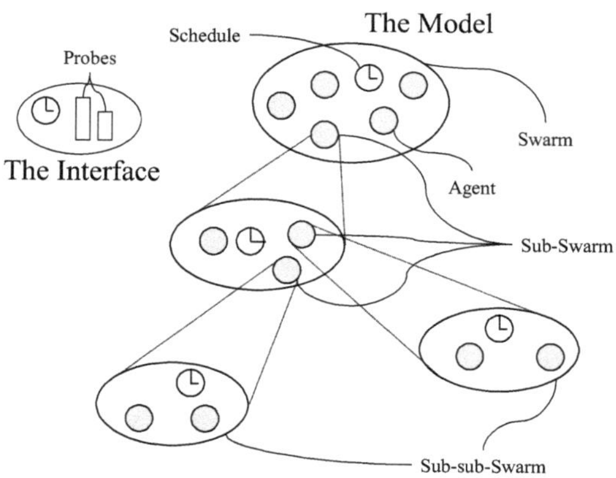

Figure 4-3 The Swarm's nested inherent hierarchical structure

JADE and FIPA

JADE (Java Agent DEvelopment Framework, http://sharon.cselt.it/projects/jade/) is a physical multi-agent development framework which complies with FIPA specifications and aims at simplifying the implementation of multi-agent systems. JADE includes two main products: an FIPA-compliant agent platform and a package to develop Java agents. The advantages of utilizing JADE as a physical agent platform include its capabilities to distribute agents across different operating platforms and to make these agents easily communicate with each other through the Internet. Besides, it can simply integrate with existing systems or databases, and provide graphical interfaces for users to manage their agents.

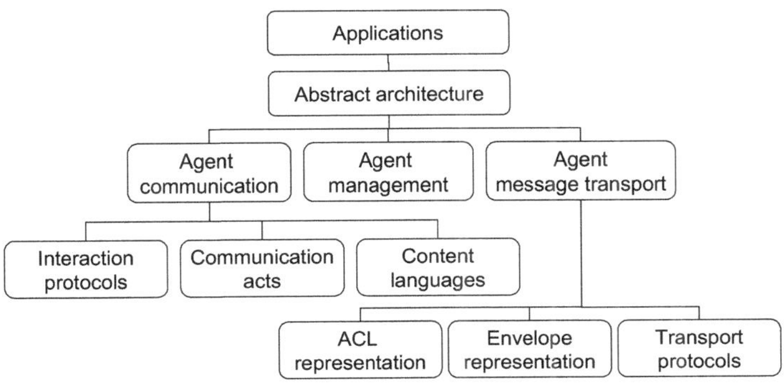

Figure 4-4 FIPA Specification

The efforts of developing physical agent as software systems are firstly summarized as distributed artificial intelligence in Bond and Gasser's book (1988), and the inter-operability of the multi-agent systems across the Internet has been initiated by the Foundation for Intelligent Physical Agents (FIPA, http://www.fipa.org) in 1996. FIPA was formed to produce software standards for heterogeneous agent-based systems. Many publicly available implementations of the agent platforms conform to FIPA specifications, such as FIPA-OS, JADE, et cetera. Figure 4-4 illustrates the building layers of the physical agents complying with FIPA standards (http://www.fipa.org). FIPA application specifications are example application areas in which FIPA agents can be deployed. They represent ontology and service specifications for a particular domain. In Figure 4-4, the FIPA abstract architecture specifications describe the abstract entities that are required to build agent services and environments. FIPA agent communication specifications define Agent Communication Language (ACL) messages, message exchange interaction protocols, speech act theory-based communicative acts and content language representations. FIPA agent management specifications define the control and management of agents within and across agent platforms. FIPA agent message transport specifications define the transport and representation of messages across different network transport protocols, including wire and wireless environments.

The implementations of simulated agents on the Swarm platform and the physical agents on the JADE platform are shown in Figure 4-1.

Chapter 5 2S-DORA: Two Stage Distributed Optimality Reaching Approach

This chapter presents a two-stage optimization approach 2S-DORA, which can be applied to solve the MCDCOP. The 2S-DORA is developed based on the derived requirements in Section 3.5. To solve an MCDCOP is to find a set of values for variables to not only consistently satisfy the inter-agent constraints but also optimize agents' objective functions. In the problem, since no agent has an overall view of the whole problem, traditional approaches to solving constraint optimization problem is unable to handle it, and a new technique is required.

This chapter begins by introducing a simple multi-objective DCOP and demonstrating how the problem is solved in Section 5.1. Section 5.2 then extends the problem-solving concept to develop 2S-DORA to further solve a multi-objective context-dependent DCOP. In order to facilitate the activity coordination in the mobile environment, Section 5.3 designs a reservation exchange protocol for mobile users to communicate with each other to resolve the distributed conflicts. Finally in Section 5.4, how the 2S-DORA and the reservation exchange protocol take advantage of the SPA framework and how they operate on the SPA are presented.

5.1 Demonstration of Solving Multi-objective DCOP

Figure 5-1(a) introduces a simple multi-objective DCOP with four variables x_1, x_2, x_{12} and x_{21}. In this problem, x_1 and x_2 are two independent variables. They are respectively controlled by the agents a_1 and a_2. The x_{12} and x_{21} are shared variables between a_1 and a_2. In this problem, a_1 and a_2 have their personal cost functions f_1 and f_2. The a_1's and a_2's objectives are to determine the values of their controlled variables so as to minimize their own cost. The values of variables (x_1, x_{12}) and (x_2, x_{21}) are respectively the policies of a_1 and a_2. The $x_{12} = x_{21}$ in Figure 5-1(a) is an external constraint to a_1 and a_2. To solve this problem is to search for an optimal policy combination for the agents.

In this problem, we assume that a_1 pursues its personal objective prior to a_2 and get its policy $(x_1, x_{12}) = (0, 0)$ as shown in Figure 5-1(b). In Figure 5-1(b), a_1 has reached its optimality. Afterward, a_2 pursues its personal objective as shown in Figure 5-1(c), where x_2 is set to be 1 subject to the shared constraint $x_{12} = x_{21}$. Its policy $(x_2, x_{21}) = (1, 0)$.

As soon as a_2 gets its policy (1, 0), a_2 ignores its worse policies, such as (0, 0) and (0, 1), and memorizes the better policy (1, 1). For a_2, if we compare the better policy (1, 1) with its current policy (1, 0), we will find that the values of x_{21} in these two policies are different. If x_{21} can be changed to be 1, the cost function f_2 will be 0 and a_2 will get its optimal policy. To change the value of x_{21}, a_2 must send a request message to a_1 to ask for the value change from 0 to 1 because x_{12} is a shared constraint between them. a_1, once receiving the request message, will assess the effect of the value change of x_{12}. We assume that if the value change harms a_1's interests, a_1 will reject the request. Otherwise, a_1 will accept the request and return an accept message as shown in Figure 5-1(d). After x_{12}'s value has been changed, a_2 will ignore the policy (0, 1) and its policy will be updated to be (1, 1). Besides, a_1's policy will be updated to be (0, 1) as shown in Figure 5-1(e). In Figure 5-1(e), the agents' policy combination is in a stable and equilibrium state since no improvement can be further made.

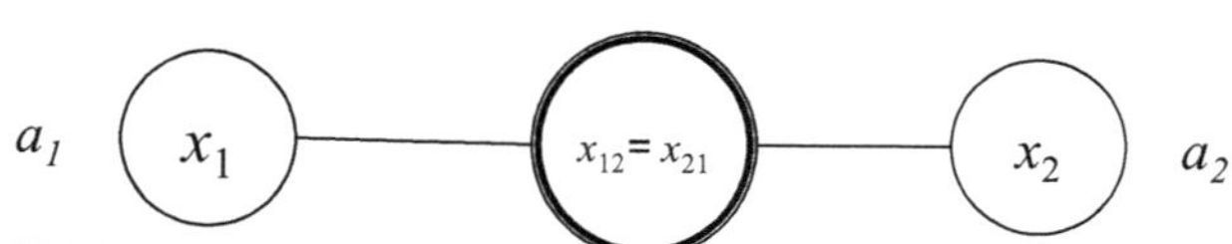

x_1	x_{12}	$f_1(x_1,x_{12})$
0	0	0
0	1	0
1	0	1
1	1	2

x_2	x_{21}	$f_2(x_2,x_{21})$
0	0	2
0	1	1
1	0	1
1	1	0

Figure 5-1(a) A simple multi-objective DCOP

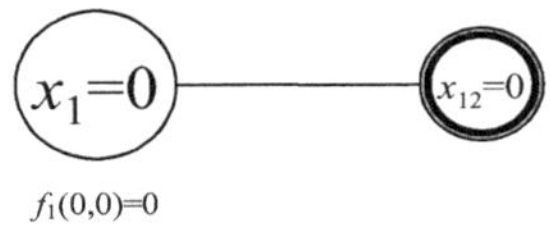

Figure 5-1(b) a_1's optimal policy

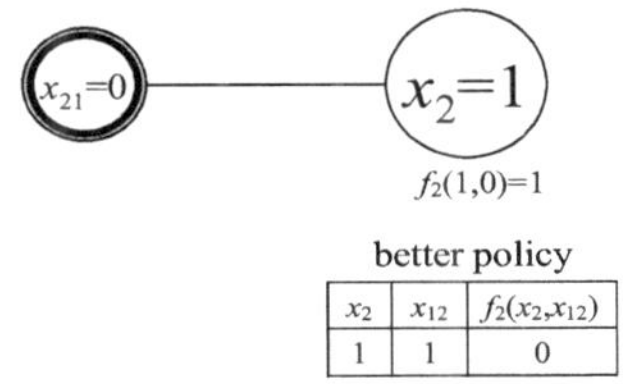

Figure 5-1(c) a_2's optimal policy subject to x_{21}

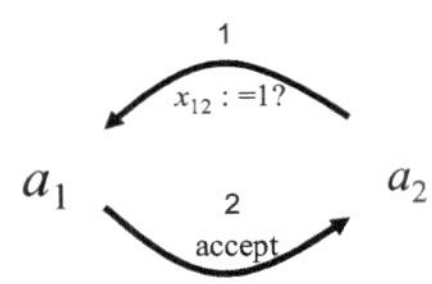

Figure 5-1(d) Coordination on the shared variable x_{12} to improve a_2's policy

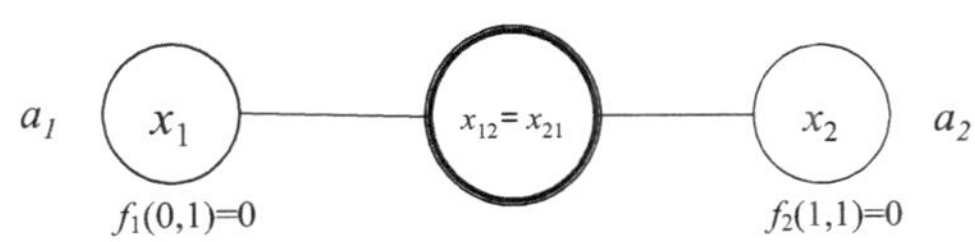

Figure 5-1(e) Optimal combination of agents' policies

Figure 5-1 Demonstration of solving a simple multi-objective DCOP

5.2 Development of 2S-DORA

Figure 5-2 shows the flowchart of the 2S-DORA. At its first stage, the 2S-DORA applies the forward chaining method to help every mobile user search for his/her personal constrained optimal solution. Thereafter, at its second stage, the 2S-DORA applies the cooperative improvement method to help mobile users improve their solutions. The cooperative improvement method uses a pre-designed decentralized coordination mechanism to support individuals in organizing coordination networks to cooperatively improving their policies. In order to avoid the improvement inconsistencies, we use state shifts to regulate mobile users' behaviors. When a user is using the 2S-DORA, his/her state will shift as shown in Figure 5-2. The state shifts will be explained later in this section and in Figure 5-5.

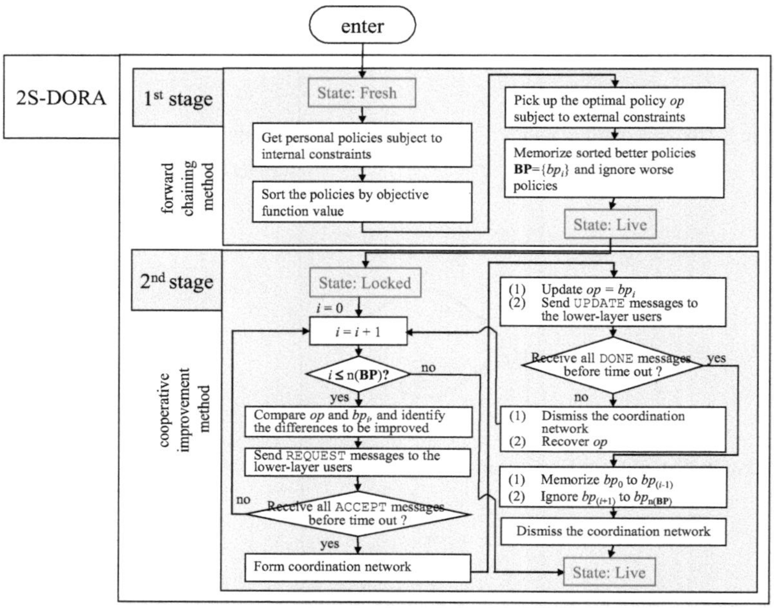

Figure 5-2 Flowchart of 2S-DORA

At the first stage, the forward chaining method does the following tasks. First, the method identifies the feasible solution space by obeying the state-shift rules and subject to the internal constraints. Second, the method sorts the feasible solutions from best to worst according to their objective function values. Third, the method checks the sorted solutions top down to pick up the optimal one subject to the external constraints.

After obtaining the optimal solution, which stands for the personal optimal policy, the method does the following three things. First, it assigns values to the variables according to the optimal policy and second, it memorizes the better policies (than the optimal one) in his/her working memory and ignores the worse ones. The 2S-DORA will later use the memorized policies to improve the user's personal optimal policy at the second stage. Third, the user's state will shift from 'Fresh' to

‘Live’. A ‘Live’ user can enter the second stage to improve his/her policy or to help the other users improve their policies.

At the second stage of the 2S-DORA, the cooperative improvement method runs on a pre-designed decentralized coordination mechanism. A user, if s/he has better policies in his/her working memory and wants to improve his/her policy, can initiate and invite related users to organize a coordination network. The related users don’t have to know each other. They are those who share the variables in the to-be-improved policy with the network initiator. The mechanism, which guides the related users to organize networks, is a virtually built mechanism in the distributed environment. The network is a virtual, temporary, self-organized and loosely-coupled organization.

Coordination network

The topology of the coordination network is a tree-structured graph which is distributed, directed and acyclic. In the network, any user can have at most one parent user and many child users. The 2S-DORA calls the parent the upper-layer user and the child the lower-layer user. In the network, users exchange necessary information to change the values of their common variables to improve their joint policies.

The cooperative improvement method will terminate the temporarily organized coordination network once its mission is completed or fails or when the network operates over a preset time period. If the method can make no improvement for the users’ policy combination, the whole distributed environment will be in a stable state. A stable environment will always maintain stable unless the environmental context varies or an exception happens.

Figure 5-3(a) shows a simple coordination network for the example in Section 3-2-2, where user #3 improves his/her schedule by exchanging reservations with user #2. User #2 exchanges reservations with user #1. User #3 initiates the coordination network, which connects user #1, #2, #3 as shown in Figure 5-3(a). The network consists of two portions that are circled by the dashed-lines. The first portion contains users #3 and #2, and the second portion contains users #2 and #1. In this network, user #3 only interacts with #2, user #2 interacts with users #3 and #1, and user #1 interacts with user #2. Mobile user #3 will not directly interact with #1. In this network, user #3 is called the upper-layer user of user #2 and user #2 the lower-layer user of user #3. In Figure 5-3(a), the network is to be terminated after the exchanges are completed. Figure 5-3(b) shows another coordination network, which consists of four portions, is more complicated than that in Figure 5-3(a).

In the distributed environment, more than one coordination network can operate simultaneously, but at the same time a user can at most join a network. That is, when a user joins a coordination network, s/he is not allowed to join another one until his/her involved coordination network is terminated and dismissed. This restriction can avoid the inconsistencies when the users are interacting with each other to change values of variables.

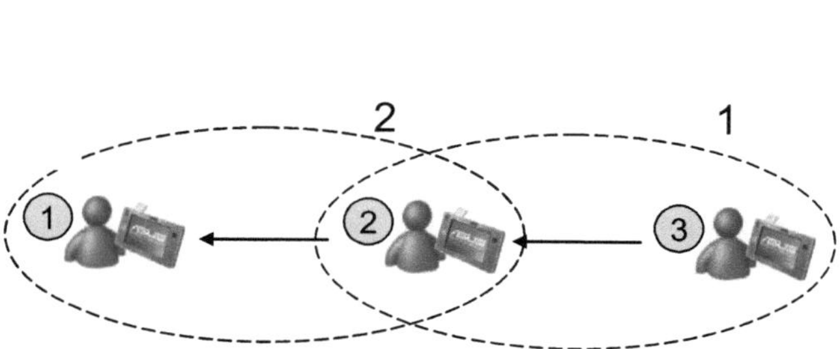

Figure 5-3(a) Coordination network of the example in Section 3-2-2

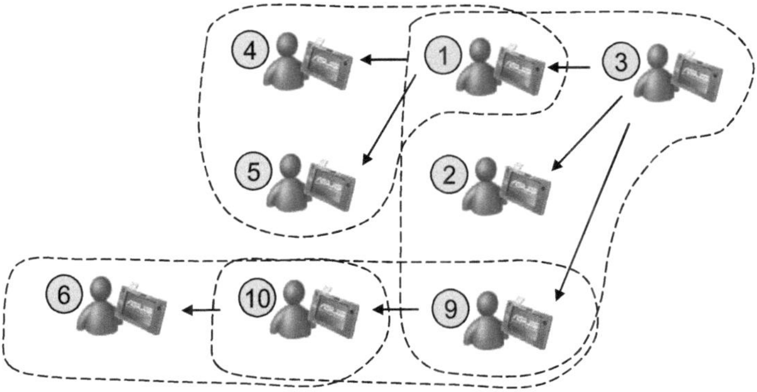

Figure 5-3(b) a complicated coordination network

Figure 5-3 Coordination networks formed by decentralized coordination mechanism

Communication performatives

In order to help mobile users express their intentions when they are communicating with each other, eight communication performatives, including `REQUEST`, `ACCEPT`, `REJECT`, `DISMISS`, `DONE`, `UPDATE`, `QUERY` and `RESPONSE`, are defined. The communication performatives are mobile users' communicative acts as shown in Figure 5-4. The `REQUEST` is used when a user intends to initialize a network. The `ACCEPT/REJECT` is used when a user intends to accept or reject the requests from his/her upper-layer user. The `UPDATE` is used when a user intends to inform his/her lower-layer users to update their schedules. The `DONE` is used to notify the upper-layer user when s/he has updated his/her schedule. The `DISMISS` is used when a mobile user intends to dismiss or terminate his/her initialized coordination network. The `QUERY` is used when a user intends to query the reservation condition of a service provider. The `RESPONSE` is used when a service provider response his/her reservation condition to a user.

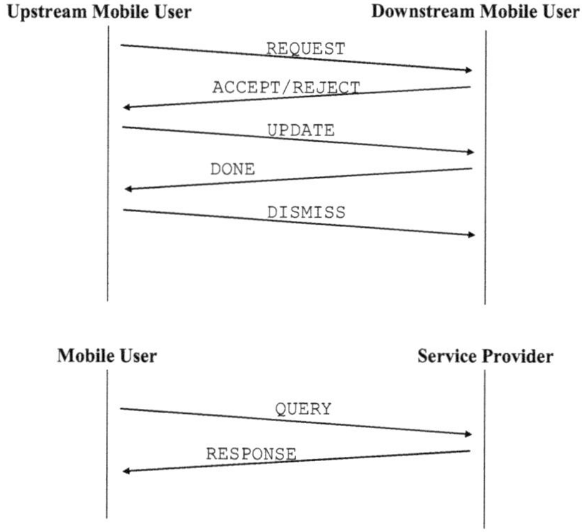

Figure 5-4 Communication performatives between the users

To improve personal policies, as the cooperative improvement method shown in Figure 5-2, a user should follow the following nine steps:

1. Shift his/her state to the locked state. During the locked state, the user is not allowed to join any other coordination networks.
2. Select one in a descending order from the better policies stored in working memory until each one of them has been tried out or the user's policy has been successfully improved. The selected policy serves as the goal for the user to achieve during a coordination process.
3. Identify the variables which differentiate the selected policy from the existing one by comparing the two policies. The identified variables will be updated in the following steps.
4. Send `QUERY` message to service providers to get the identities of lower-layer users with interrelated variables, and expect to receive `RESPONSE` messages from these service providers.

5. Send `REQUEST` messages to the lower-layer users to initialize a coordination network. The `REQUEST` messages contain the interrelated variables with corresponding values discovered in Step 3.
6. If all the lower-layer users return `ACCEPT` messages before the timeout, a coordination network is born. Otherwise, try other better policies or terminate the improvement request cycle.
7. Update the policies by sending `UPDATE` messages to the lower-layer users requesting value adjustment for interrelated variables.
8. If all of the lower-layer users echo with `DONE` messages before the timeout, the improvement is successfully made. The user then records the updated policy, discards worse policies from working memory, and dismisses the coordination network. Otherwise, the user will restore its original policy and dismiss the coordination network.
9. Once the coordination network is dismissed, the locked users will return to the live state.

Figure 5-5 shows a user's response when s/he receives different messages in the network. Figure 5-5(a) is the `REQUEST` message, Figure 5-5(b) the `ACCEPT` message, Figure 5-5(c) the `REJECT` message, Figure 5-5(d) the `UPDATE` message, Figure 5-5(e) the `DONE` message, and Figure 5-5(f) the `DISMISS` message.

In Figure 5-5(a), upon receiving a `REQUEST` message, a user whose state is live, will assess the effect of value changes on corresponding variables. If the assessment indicates that the changes are beneficial or harmless, the user will accept the request, and echo upper-layer users with an `ACCEPT` message. If the assessment shows that the user's utility will diminish, the user will further try to help its upper-layer user satisfy the request. The user first pushes its current policy into its working memory, and then, assuming the values of the corresponding variables have changed, tries to improve the changed policy by following the aforementioned nine steps. If the changed policy cannot improve the utility, the agent will restore its original policy and then echo with a `REJECT` message to its upper-layer user.

In Figure 5-5(b), upon receiving an `ACCEPT` message, a user will first check whether all requests are accepted. If not all requests are returned, the user stores the `ACCEPT` message for later checking. If all requests are accepted and the user has an upper-layer user, s/he will return an `ACCEPT` message to the upper-layer user. If all requests are accepted and the user has no upper-layer user, the coordination network will be formed and the user will update his/her policy and send a `UPDATE` message to his/her lower-layer users.

In Figure 5-5(c), upon receiving a `REJECT` message, a user will return a `REJECT` message to his/her upper-layer user if there is any or send a `DISMISS` message to its lower-layer users if there is none.

In Figure 5-5(d), upon receiving a `UPDATE` message, a user will update his/her policy. In addition, the user will forward `UPDATE` messages to his/her lower-layer users if there is any. Otherwise, the user will return a `DONE` message to his/her upper-layer user.

In Figure 5-5(e), upon receiving a `DONE` message, a user will first check whether all `DONE` messages are returned. If not all `DONEs` are returned, the user stores the message for later checking. If all `DONE`s are returned and there is an upper-layer user, the agent will return a `DONE` message to it. If all `DONE`s are returned and there is no upper-layer user, the user will send `DISMISS` messages to its lower-layer users to dismiss the coordination network.

In Figure 5-5(f), upon receiving a `DISMISS` message, a user will forward `DISMISS` messages to his/her lower-layer users if there is any and dismiss his/her coordination network.

The assessment of changing the values of common variables follows the premises of Pareto improvement to determine whether the value changes are at least weakly beneficial, namely, with no worse outcome. Moreover, the change of variables' values obeys the "all or nothing" rule; that is, if anyone in the coordination network refuses to change the variable values, the improvement fails, and the coordination network will be terminated.

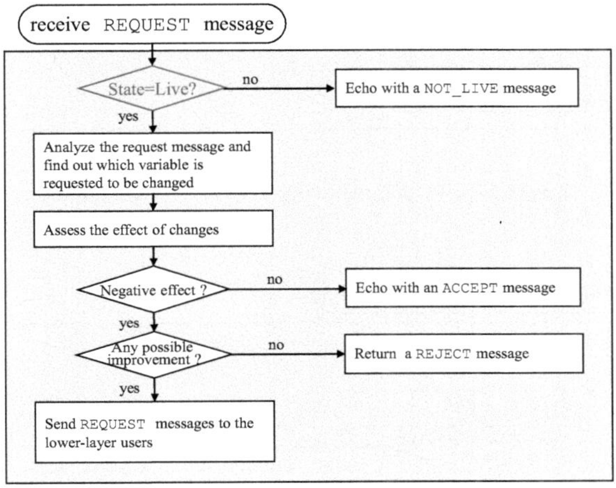

Figure 5-5(a) Upon receiving a REQUEST message

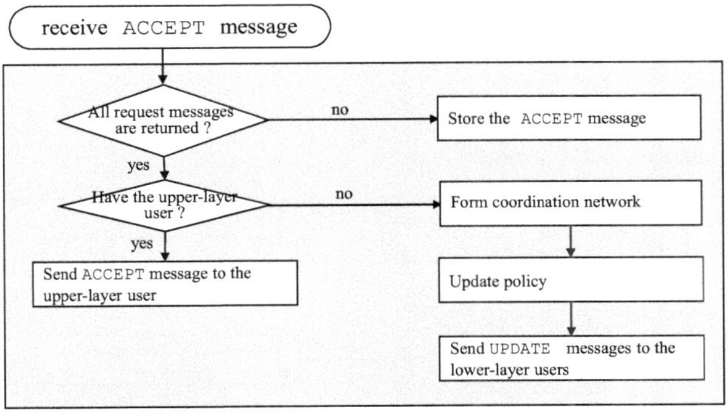

Figure 5-5(b) Upon receiving an ACCEPT message

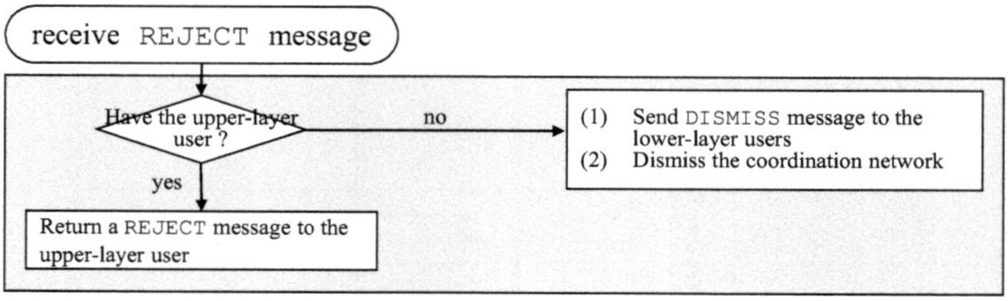

Figure 5-5(c) Upon receiving a REJECT message

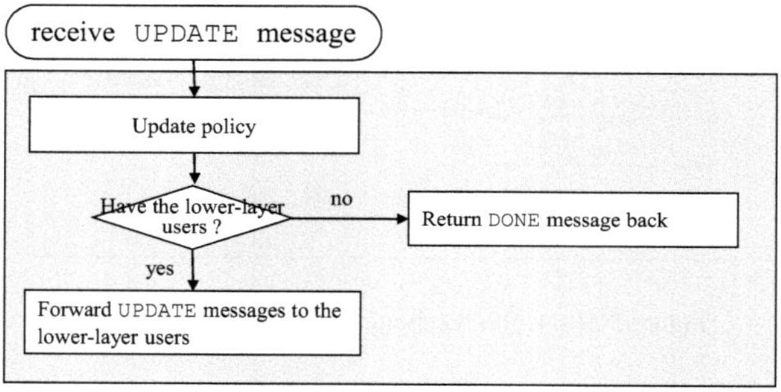

Figure 5-5(d) Upon receiving an UPDATE message

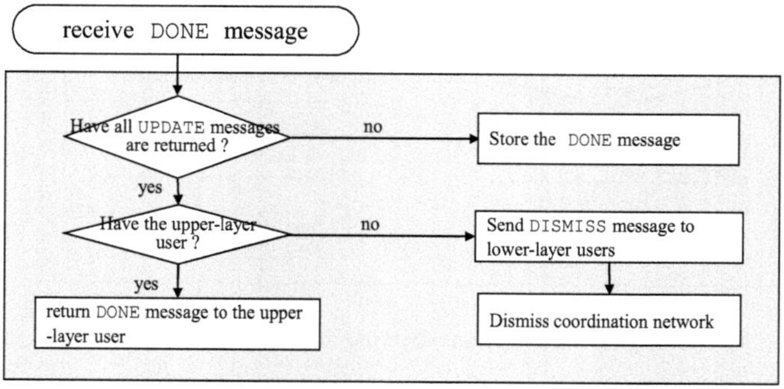

Figure 5-5(e) Upon receiving a DONE message

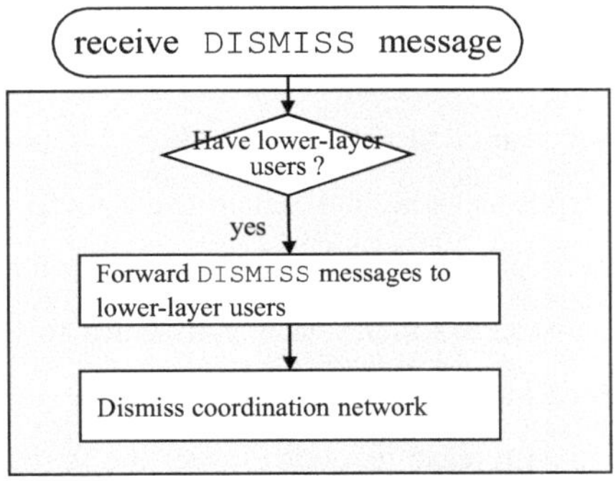

Figure 5-5(f) Upon receiving a DISMISS message

Figure 5-5 A user's reaction upon receiving messages

Users' State Diagram

To ensure that a user can initialize a coordination network or is ready to join any coordination network, a state diagram is introduced to regulate a user's behaviors. A user in the distributed environment can be in one of the five states as the state diagram shows in Figure 5-6. The five states are fresh, live, locked, solitary and off-line. Figure 5-2 and 5-5 shows the state shifts when a user is obtaining and improving his/her policy. The following explains the five states.

1. Fresh: Any user enters the mobile environment in the fresh state. Once the user subsequently plans his/her personal policy and obtains his/her personal policy, s/he will enter the live state. If a fresh user decides to leave the environment, s/he will enter the off-line state.
2. Live: Any live user can use the coordination mechanism to cooperate with others to improve his/her own policy or other users' policies. On joining a coordination network, a live user will enter the locked state. It can also enter the solitary state if s/he refuses to interact with others or enter the off-line state if s/he decides to leave the mobile environment.
3. Locked: A locked user is the one that interacts with its upper- or lower-layer users in the coordination network they make up. None of the locked users can join any other coordination network until the dismissal of the operating

coordination network. A locked user returns to the live state as soon as the operating coordination network is dismissed.

4. Solitary: If a user wants to re-plan or adjust its policy due to contextual variations or exceptions, s/he will enter the solitary state. A solitary user refuses to interact with other users, and will not initiate or join any coordination networks. A solitary user can return to the live state once s/he completes his/her re-planning or adjustment.
5. Off-line: A user must release its control over the variables before leaving the mobile environment when s/he enters the off-line state.

The pseudo code of the 2S-DORA is shown in Figure 5-7.

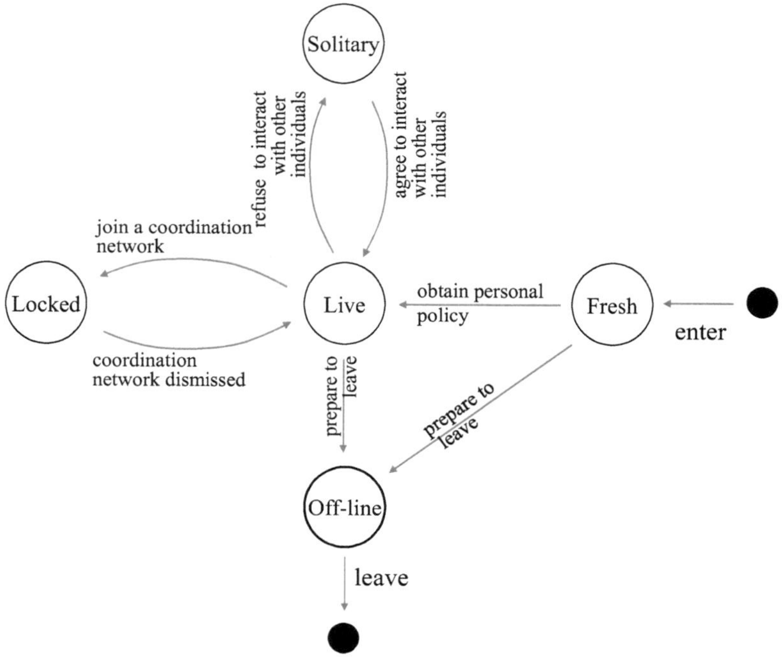

Figure 5-6 Users' state diagram

2S-DORA

```
Given
internal_constraint;
external_constraint;
objective_function;

Initialize
available_policy:={};
sorted_avaliable_poliy:={};
optimal_policy:=null;
better_policy:={};
state:='Fresh'

available_policy:= getPersonalPolicySubject2InternalConstraint (
                        internal_constraint);
sorted_avaliable_policy := sortPolicyByObjectiveFunctionValue (available_policy,
                        objective_function);
optimal_policy := pickUpOptimalPolicySubject2ExternalConstraint (
                        sorted_avaliable_policy, external_constraint);
better_policy := getBetterPolicy (sorted_avaliable_policy, optimal_policy);
state :=' Live'
state :=' Locked'
optimal_policy := improveOptimalPolicy (state, optimal_policy,
          better_policy);
better_policy := getResidualBetterPolicy (better_policy, optimal_policy);
state :=' Live'
```

```
procedure optimal_policy improveOptimalPolicy (state, optimal_policy,
               better_policy) {
 op := optimal_policy;
  improved:=false;
  i:=0;
  if (state =' Locked') {
   do {
        i := i + 1;
        bp := get i^th policy in better_policy;
        difference := getDifferenceBetweenOptimalPolicyAndBetterPolicy (optimal_policy,
                             bp);
     sendRequestMessage2LowerLayerUser (difference);
        result := waitToReceiveAccept();
     if (result) {
        lowerLayerUser := getLowerLayerUsers (difference);
       op := bp;
       sendUpdateMessage2LowerLayerUser(lowerLayerUser);
               improved := waitToReceiveDone();
               if (improved) dismissCoordinationNetwork (lowerLayerUser);
              }
        }
   }
   until all better_policy tried or improved=true;
    state :=' Live';
  }
  return op;
}
```

```
procedure better_policies getResidualBetterPolicy (better_policy, optimal_policy) {
  bp={};
  i := 0;
  do {
      i := i + 1;
    p := get i^th better_policy;
    if p is better than optimal_policy {
       add p to bp;
    }
   }
  until p equals optimal_policy;
  return bp;
}
```

```
procedure difference getDifferenceBetweenOptimalPolicyAndBetterPolicy (optimal_policy,
              better_policy) {
   difference := {};
  i := 0;
  do {
      i := i + 1;
      op_elem := get i^th element of optimal_policy;
      bp_elem := get the same element in better_policy ;
      if (value(op_elem) != value(bp_elem))
     add bp_elem to difference;
  }
  return difference;
}
```

```
procedure sendRequestMessage2LowerLayerUser (difference) {
  i := 0;
  do {
      i := i + 1;
      diff_elem := get i^th element of difference;
      p := individual with whom diff_elem is shared;
    send diff_elem to p;
  }
}
```

```
procedure result waitToReceiveAccept (msg) {
 do {
     if all msg are ACCEPT {
       result := true;
       return result;
   }
     else if time out {
        result := false;
        return result;
     }
     else if any msg is REJECT or NOT_LIVE {
        result := false;
        return result;
```

```
        }
    }
}
```

```
procedure result waitToReceiveDone (msg) {
  do {
      if all msg are DONE {
         result := true;
         return result;
     }
        else if time out {
           result := false;
           return result;
        }
    }
}
```

```
procedure user getLowerLayerUsers (difference) {
   user := {};
  i := 0;
  do {
        i := i + 1;
        diff_elem := get i^th element of difference;
        p := user with whom diff_elem is shared;
     add p to user;
  }
   return user;
}
```

```
procedure dismissCoordinationNetwork (user) {
   send DISMISS message to all lower-layer users;
}
```

```
procedure sendUpdateMessage2LowerLayerUser(user) {
   send UPDATE message to all User;
}
```

```
procedure sendDismissMessage2LowerLayerUser(user) {
   send DISMISS message to all user;
}
```

```
procedure available_policy getPersonalPolicySubject2InternalConstraint
     (internal_constraint) {
  ap:={ };
  forall policy_i if policy_i satisfied with internal_constraint
     add policy_i to ap;
   return ap;
}
```

```
procedure sorted_avaliable_policy sortPolicyByObjectiveFunctionValue
    (available_policy,objective-function) {
   sap:= sort available_policy by referring to objective-function;
   return sap;
}
```

```
procedure optimal_policy pickUpOptimalPolicySubject2ExternalConstraint
    (sorted_avaliable_policy, external_constraint) {
  satisfied= false;
  i := 0;
  op = null;
  do {
      i := i + 1;
    soa := get i^th policy in sorted_avaliable_policy;
    if soa is satisfied with external_constraint {
      satisfied = true;
          op := soa;
    }
  }
  until satisfied;
  return op;
}
```

```
procedure better_policy getBetterPolicy (sorted_avaliable_policy, optimal_policy)
    {
  bp :={ };
  i := 0;
  do {
      i := i + 1;
    soa := get i^th sorted_avaliable_policy;
    if soa is better than optimal_policy {
      add soa to bp;
    }
  }
  until (soa=optimal_policy);
  return bp;
}
```

```
proceduce effect analyze&assess (msg, objective-function) {
      effect := false;
    if request in msg do no harm effect := true;
    if request in msg benefits effect := true;
    return effect;
}
```

```
Upon receiving REQUEST message msg
  bp := null;
  If (state != 'Live') {
     feed back NOT_LIVE message;
  } else {
     state := 'Locked';
```

```
effect := analyze&assess (msg);
if (effect) feed back ACCEPT message;
 else {
   np := a new policy by assuming that REQUEST msg is accepted;
    add optimal_policy to better_policy;
do {
      i := i + 1;
      bp := get i^th policy in better_policy;
      difference := getDifferenceBetweenOptimalPolicyAndBetterPolicy (optimal_policy,
                          np);
 sendRequestMessage2LowerLayerUser (difference);
      result := waitToReceiveAccept();
 if (result) {
            individual := getLowerLayerUsers (difference);
            op := bp;
            sendUpdateMessage2LowerLayerUser(individual);
             improved := waitToReceiveDone();
             if (improved) dismissCoordinationNetwork (individual);
            }
      }
}
until all better_policy tried out or improved=true;
     if (!improved ) echo REJECT message;
 }
}
}
```

```
Upon receiving UPDATE message msg
   optimal_policy := bp;
   if (individual is null) {
        return DONE message
   }
   else {
    sendUpdateMessage2LowerLayerUser(individual);
   }
}
```

```
Upon receiving ACCEPT message msg
   if all update messages are returned {
      if upper-layer user exists {
        send ACCEPT message to upper-layer user;
       }
      else {
        optimal_policy := bp;
        sendUpdateMessage2LowerLayerUser (user);
      }
   }
   else {
     store the msg for later checking;
   }
}
```

```
Upon receiving DONE message msg
```

```
        if all request messages are returned {
           if upper-layer user exists {
              return DONE  message to upper-layer user;
           }
           else {
            sendDismissMessage2LowerLayerUser(user);
           }
        }
        else {
           store the msg for later checking;
        }
    }
```

```
Upon receiving REJECT message msg
        if upper-layer user exists {
          return REJECT message to upper-layer user;
        }
        else {
          sendDismissMessage2LowerLayerUser(user);
        }
    }
```

```
Upon receiving DISMISS message msg
   dismissCoordinationNetwork (user);
```

Figure 5-7 Pseudo code of 2S-DORA

Reservation exchange scheme

In the 2S-DORA, the value changes of variables by the cooperative improvement method are the reservation exchanges among the mobile users. The reservation exchanges can be initiated when a user memorizes better schedule(s) and wants to improve his/her schedule, or when a user's objective or schedule is impacted by a context variation or an exception, or when any improvement over their joint schedules is possible or is required.

A mobile user, when s/he wants to improve his/her schedule, must develop his/her reservation exchange schemes by following the procedures below and run the schemes:

1. Compare the differences between his/her schedule and the better schedule s/he wants to transform into. Identify the reservations corresponding to the differences, which are the targets to be exchanged.

2. Query the service providers about who owns the reservations.
3. Develop a reservation exchange scheme. The scheme describes the process to exchange reservations and which reservation can be exchanged with whom.
4. Translate the scheme into `REQUEST` messages referring to the reservation exchange protocol. The `REQUEST` messages will be sequentially sent to his/her lower-layer users in a unicast mode to form coordination network.

Figure 5-8 shows an example in which mobile user #90 tries to improve his/her schedule from M[1]C[4]P[7], *i.e.*, visiting the 1st M, the 4th C and finally the 7th P, to P[1]C[4]L[4]M[5]. M, C, P, and L are the providers of on-site services.

To make the improvement, user #90 first analyzes the differences between his/her schedule and the better schedule. The differences contain P[1→7], M[5→1], and L[4]. After identifying the differences, user #90 develops reservation exchange schemes. There might be many possible schemes to run. For example, the user can make new reservations L[4], P[7], and M[1] and release owned reservations P[1], and M[5]. If this scheme works, the user successfully improve his/her schedule. Otherwise, the user will try another scheme. Figure 5-8 demonstrates an alternative reservation exchange scheme as follows: reserve a new L[4], exchange P[1] with someone to get P[7] and exchange M[5] with someone to get M[1]. To check whether the exchanges are workable, the user develops a reservation exchange scheme by first querying the service providers about who owns those reservations. Afterward, s/he sends the `REQUEST` messages to the owners, *e.g.*, user #5, to invite them to form a coordination network. If the new reservation and the reservation exchanges works, the user successfully improve his/her schedule. Otherwise, user #90 can attempt to form an alternative network with some other users, *e.g.*, with mobile user #5 and #7. An invited user, once receiving a `REQUEST` message, and the request reducing his/her satisfaction, will develop his/her reservation exchange schemes to improve the assumed new schedule (after exchanges) to at least remain his/her original satisfaction.

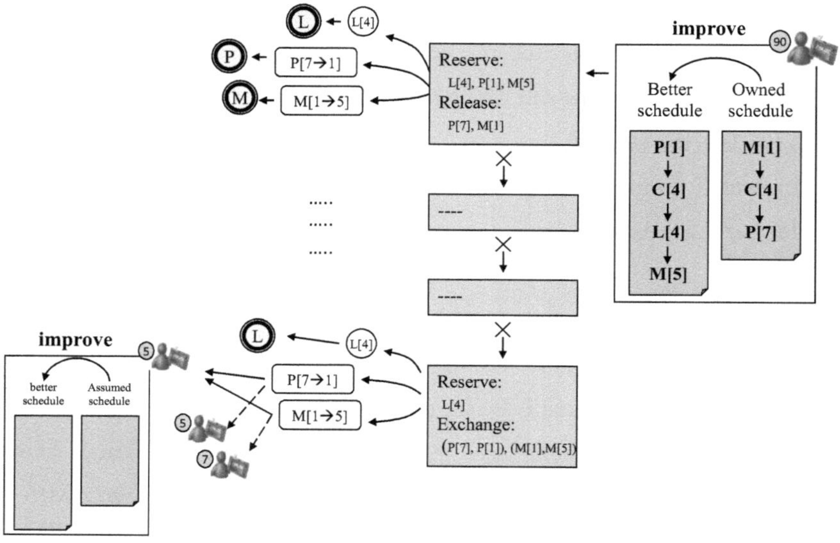

Figure 5-8 An example of developing reservation exchange scheme

In the MUCP, the joint optimality is achieved and the mobile environment reaches a state of equilibrium if there is no reservation cancellation, no context variation, no exception, and no possible improvement over users' schedules.

5.3 Reservation Exchange Protocol

Mobile users' reservation exchanges conform to the reservation exchange protocol. The protocol defines the communication language, the communication performatives and the reservation exchange rules for physical agents to interact with each other and to arrive at a compromise on their exchanges. The communication language is a predefined message format used for users' agents to communicate with each other. The performatives follow the definitions in Section 5-2 and in Figure 5-4. The reservation exchange rules are those for users to effectively exchange their reservations.

Mobile users interact with each other by exchanging messages. Their messages are coded referring to a common communication language. We develop the language based on the communication ontology shown in Figure 5.8. Ontology is the specification of a conceptualization (Gruber, 1993), which describes the concepts, the concepts' attributes and the relations between the concepts. The ontology contains eight concepts, including Service Provider, Mobile User, Service, Activity Reservation, Condition Query, Reservation Condition, Exchange and Cancellation. In Figure 5.9, we implement the ontology as a communication language to endow the SPA's physical agents with the social abilities.

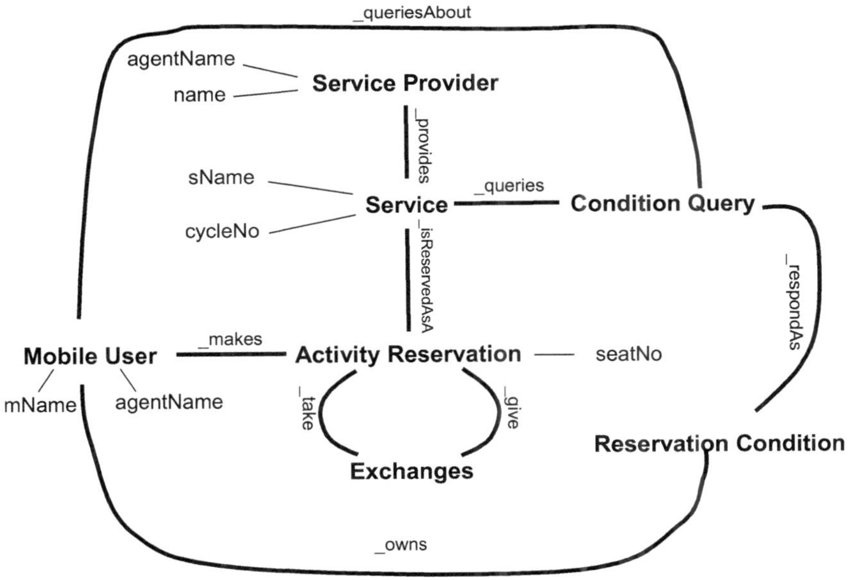

Figure 5-9 Communication ontology

We regard the reservation exchanges of mobile activities for coordination as a series of social exchanges. The rules for the exchanges are based on the social exchange theory that every mobile user will evaluate the reward and cost of every reservation request, and then decide its acceptance or rejection. A mobile user will accept an exchange if s/he benefits from the exchange or at least sacrifice nothing from the exchange.

All of the mobile users are equal in the mobile environment. Thus, everyone can initiate his/her coordination network. More than one coordination network can operate independently and simultaneously, but no one can join more than one network at the same time. A coordination network is effective before its initiator dismisses it. Besides, a coordination network will be automatically terminated if it operates over a preset time period. The above-mentioned rules can increase the efficiency of the reservation exchanges and can avoid the inconsistencies among users' schedules. However, the rules induce a new problem that if too many users initiate their coordination networks, their states will shift from the live state to the locked state. A locked user cannot attend any other networks. As a result, their networks will be hardly formed, and then their mobile activities will be hardly coordinated.

To ease this arising problem, our protocol adopts the Binary Exponential Backoff (BEB) algorithm to keep mobile users from successively initializing useless coordination networks. The BEB, issued by IEEE 802.3, is originally applied to schedule data retransmission after packet collisions in Ethernet. In the protocol, once a mobile user fails in organizing a coordination network, the BEB will not allow him/her to initialize another network until a time period t_c expires. t_c is a uniformly distributed random value within $(0, 2^{i-1}w)$, where i is his/her i^{th} trial to form coordination networks and w is a given value.

Furthermore, we adopts three heuristics to support mobile users in developing their reservation exchange schemes to minimize the searching cost and to make the searching time as short as possible. The first heuristic is that the smaller the number of exchanges, the more likely the reservation exchanges will succeed. This heuristic gives a reservation exchange scheme higher priority to be carried out if the scheme brings larger utility improvement with a smaller number of exchanges.

The second heuristic is that the smaller the coordination network, the more likely the reservation exchanges will succeed. This heuristic suggests that a user should invite as few users to form a coordination network as possible.

The third heuristic is that the more likely a user is to increase his/her satisfaction or at least recover his/her satisfaction to the original level, the more likely s/he will agree to join a coordination network.

The heuristics are evaluated by simulated agents in the SPA.

5.4 SPA and Built-in 2S-DORA

We implement the 2S-DORA on the SPA framework. The SPA and the built-in 2S-DORA owns the autonomic computing ability to configure and reconfigure itself under varying conditions, to act in response to the outside environment and context, and to look for ways to optimize a user's activity schedule.

The operation of the 2S-DORA on SPA is described as follows:

1. The 2S-DORA uses the social module of the SPA to exchange messages remotely. The social module of the SPA is made up of physical agents and communication ontology to send and receive messages. In the mobile environment, variables of an optimization problem are distributed, and no user can control all of the variables. The solution to the problem must be obtained by agents' interactions and message exchanges. Through message exchanges, the agents can query the service providers about their reservation conditions, to book services, to exchange reservations with others, to organize coordination networks and moreover, to solve the optimization problems. In Figure 5-10, the sequence diagrams show the agents' interactions when the users are planning or improving their schedules in the mobile environment. Figure 5-10(a) shows the agents' interactions at the 1st stage of 2S-DORA, whereas Figure 5-10(b) shows that at 2nd stage. Figure 5-10(c) demonstrates the interactions between agents when a user receives a reservation exchange request. If the context varies or an exception happens, an affected user can first re-assess his/her schedule, find better schedules, then memorize the better schedules in his/her simulated agents and finally apply the 2nd stage of 2S-DORA to improve his/her schedule.

2. The 2S-DORA uses the sensory module of the SPA to actively detect influential context variations and exceptions. The sensory module is made up of physical agents. Once a context variation or an exception is detected, the agents will update the mobile user's personal schedule. The sensory module connects a mobile users' nervous system to the environment to monitor the environmental changes.
3. The 2S-DORA embeds the reservation exchange protocol into the self-management module of the SPA to set up its decision-making rules and logics to plan, to adjust and to improve the user's schedule. The module is made up of physical agents. The agents maintain a user's state, context-dependent preferences on the services, and schedule. Plus, the agents memorize better solutions for the schedule improvement, control all of the input/output information. Moreover, the agents interact with the analytic and reasoning module, execute reservation exchange schemes, and test the effectiveness of simulated schedules by checking whether they are consistent with the shared constraints.

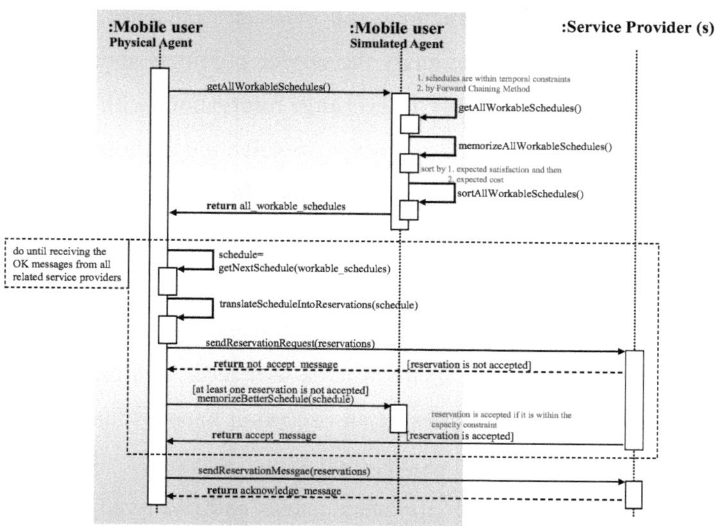

Figure 5-10(a) Plan/re-plan personal schedule (1st stage)

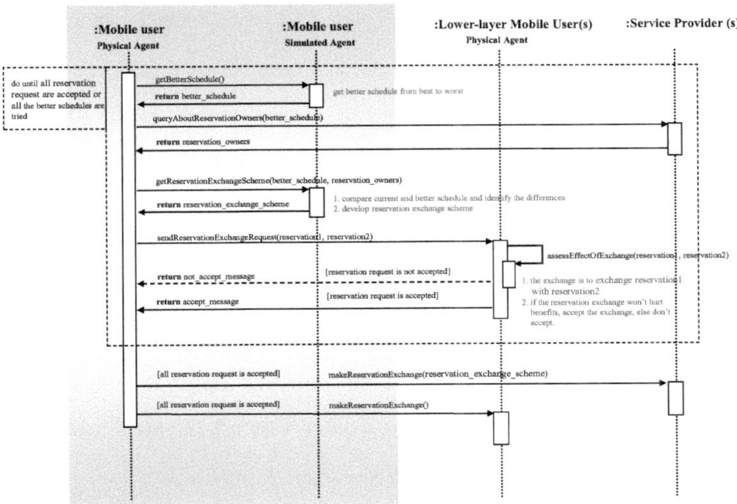

Figure 5-10(b) Improve schedules cooperatively (2nd stage)

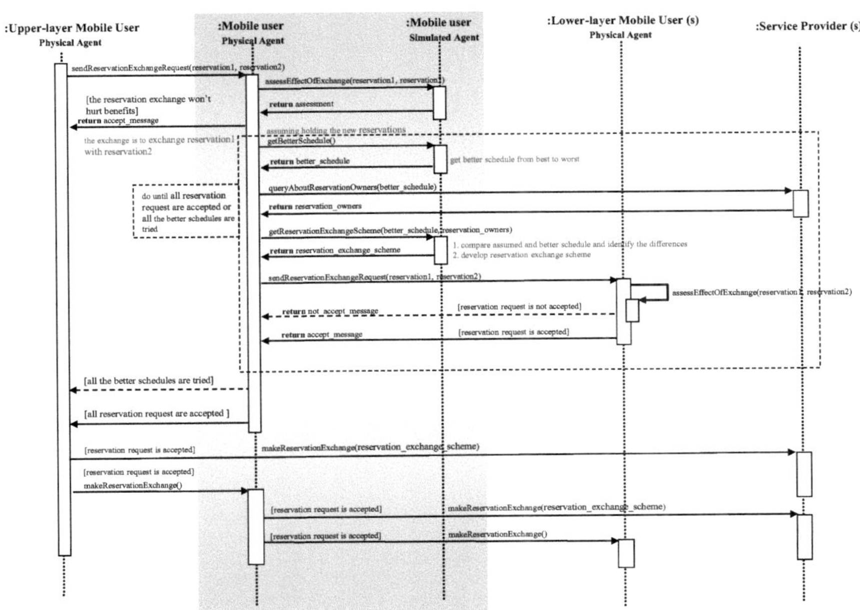

Figure 5-10(c) Upon receiving a reservation exchange request

Figure 5-10 Sequence diagrams of 2S-DORA

4. The 2S-DORA uses the analytic and reasoning module of the SPA to execute simulations. The module is made up of simulated agents, which construct a belief system. The belief system maintains a mobile user's view on the status of the mobile environment and the related users. In the module, three heuristics guide the agents to first capture the structure of the related users from the belief system and then evaluate the users' possible actions and corresponding states and to obtain the potential optimal joint actions of the users. The optimal joint actions will later support physical agents in taking actions and coordinating with others.

Chapter 6 Traveling backpacker problem

This chapter outlines an example, called traveling backpacker problem, in which many backpackers travel in a city to visit tourist attractions. The traveling backpacker problem is an extension of the MUCP investigated in Chapter 3. In this example, the SPA and its built-in 2S-DORA are applied to help backpackers plan their itineraries and coordinate their activities. We use this example later in Chapter 7 to design experiments to test the performance of SPA and its built-in 2S-DORA.

We organize this chapter as follows. Section 6.1 characterizes the traveling backpacker problem. Section 6.2 formulates the problem by extending the MUCP presented in Section 3.3.

6.1 Traveling backpacker problem

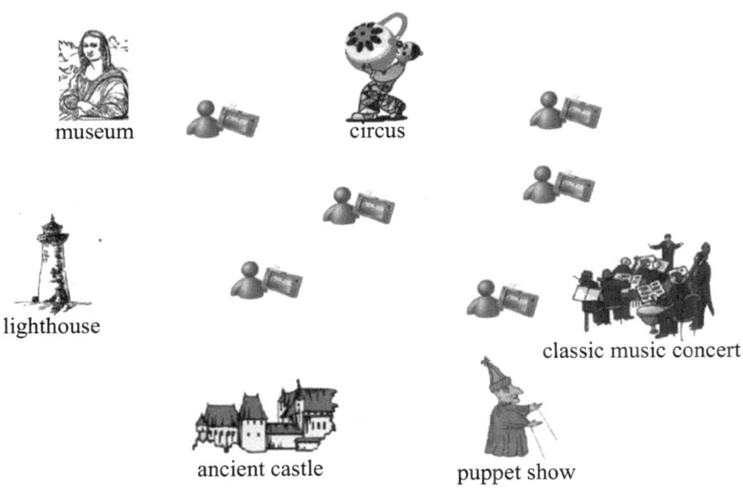

Figure 6-1 Traveling backpacker problem

In the traveling backpacker problem, backpackers and popular tourist attractions are the major players as shown in Figure 6-1. The backpackers are the global nomad

(Richards & Wilson, 2004). They are independent and autonomous travelers who walk or use public transportation to visit tourist attractions. The tourist attractions which amuse and entertain backpackers are scattered over the city. The city where the backpackers travel is a mobile city. In the city, backpackers with mobile devices can communicate with each other.

Richards and Wilson (2004) drew the characteristics of a backpacker as follows: the backpackers are independent travelers. They are cost-sensitive since they don't have sufficient budgets. They are influenced by the word-of-mouth communication in backpacker information exchange. They like to share their travel experiences and help other backpackers. They are likely to adjust their itineraries when they accept other backpackers' advice, and thus their itineraries must be flexible. Backpackers reject rigid travel timetables. They pay attentions to the preservation of their personal privacies to ensure the securities and safeties during their travels. Besides, the environment where backpackers involved in is fair; *i.e.*, all backpackers are equal, and no one owns privilege on visiting his/her designated tourist attractions.

The objective of a backpacker is to maximize his/her personal satisfaction on his/her itinerary. The satisfaction is the combination of a backpacker's utility and cost. The utility is the happiness of how much a backpacker gets, and the cost is the expense of how much s/he spends on running his/her itinerary. Therefore, during a given time period, a backpacker will gain great satisfaction if s/he visits his/her desired tourist attractions as many as possible with the required cost as less as possible.

The backpackers enter or leave the mobile city frequently. They maintain loosely-coupled relations with others. An exception may happen and backpackers' contexts may vary as time advances. The exception happening or the context variation is likely to impact backpackers' objectives and their policies to plan their personal itineraries. Therefore, the environment of the mobile city is highly dynamic and complicated. Hwang and Fesenmaier (2011) indicated that travelers will change their travel plan in response to the environmental variation so as to optimize their benefits. In such environment, conflicts among backpackers' itineraries often arise and are difficult to deal with. The travel decision-making is a complex and context-dependent process (Choe, 2014).

In this traveling backpacker problem in a mobile city, a backpacker can (1) travel without any mobile device, denoted as B1, or (2) carry a mobile device, denoted as B2, or (3) carry a SPA+2S-DORA embedded mobile device, denoted as B3. The three types of backpackers own different abilities respectively. Their abilities are shown in Table 6.1.

Table 6.1 Types of backpackers and their owned abilities

Ability \ backpacker	without any device, B1	with a pure mobile device, B2	with the SPA+ 2S-DORA, B3
Buying ticket on the spot	√	√	√
Making reservations before running itinerary		√	√
Making or canceling reservations anytime		√	√
Querying about the reservation conditions of tourist attractions anytime		√	√
Planning and adjusting the itinerary anytime		√	√
Planning and adjusting the itinerary with the assistances of multi-agents and their intelligence			√
coordinating with other backpackers at any time			√

In the traveling backpacker problem, a B3 can plan and adjust his/her itinerary with the assistance of multi-agents technologies and the developed intelligence. Moreover, s/he can make or cancel reservations, query the tourist attractions about their detailed reservation conditions and coordinate with other B3s at any time. A B2 can make or cancel reservations, and query the tourist attractions about their reservation conditions at any time. A B1 is a traditional backpacker who travels without carrying any communication device and buys tickets on the spot.

The tourist attractions serve as service providers in the MUCP. They are capacity-limited. They can only take care of certain quantity of travelers during their service time so as to maintain their service quality. Besides, in a given time period, every backpacker can visit an attraction at most once. All of the attractions are web-enabled and individually maintain their ticket reservation systems. They accept on-line reservations and reserve a percentage of tickets for locale backpackers who do not make reservations beforehand. If a backpacker wants to buy the ticket of a tourist attraction on the spot, s/he has to take the risk of unable to enjoy it.

The backpackers move from one tourist attraction to another using public transportation. We assume that the public transportation provides anytime services, and they are not capacity-limited.

6.2 Formulation of Traveling backpacker problem

We take the above-mentioned traveling backpacker problem as an extension of the MUCP. Therefore, we formulate it by slightly modifying the MUCP formulation in Section 3.3. The tourist attraction sp_i is characterized by equation 6.1, which is a modification of equation 3.3. θ in equation 6.1 denotes the percentage of tickets that tourist attraction sp_i reserves for locale backpackers. Equation 6.2, which is a modification of equation 3.12, restricts the quantity of the tickets opened for on-line reservations.

$$\mathrm{sp}_i = \mathrm{sp}_i(\mathrm{S}, \sigma, \chi, \eta, \theta) \quad (6.1)$$

$$\forall i, p \ \sum_{j=1}^{N} \mathrm{sp}_i.b_{p,j} \leq \mathrm{sp}_i.\sigma \cdot (1 - \mathrm{sp}_i.\theta) \quad (6.2)$$

The public transportation is characterized by a 2-tuple in equation 6.3. We assume that the tourist attractions are connected with each other by a set of $N \times N$ fully meshed arcs. A backpacker can use the public transportation $\kappa_{\mathrm{sp}_a,\mathrm{sp}_b}$ to move directly from one tourist attraction sp_a to the other sp_b. In equation 6.3, $\kappa_{\mathrm{sp}_a,\mathrm{sp}_b}.\mathrm{time}$

and $\kappa_{\mathrm{sp}_a,\mathrm{sp}_b}.\mathrm{cost}$ are respectively the time and cost required for any backpacker to move from sp_a to sp_b. The public transportation is symmetric $\kappa_{\mathrm{sp}_a,\mathrm{sp}_b} = \kappa_{\mathrm{sp}_b,\mathrm{sp}_a}$.

$$\kappa_{\mathrm{sp}_a,\mathrm{sp}_b} = \kappa_{\mathrm{sp}_a,\mathrm{sp}_b}(\mathrm{time},\ \mathrm{cost}) = \kappa_{\mathrm{sp}_b,\mathrm{sp}_a} \quad \text{.........(6.3)}$$

A backpacker's satisfaction is the combination of his/her utility and cost. Equation 6.4 defines a backpacker's utility, and equation 6.5 defines his/her cost. In equation 6.4, $u(\pi_t^*)$ is the expected total utility of a backpacker's optimal itinerary, and $u(\tau_i)$ is the expected utility of a backpacker's preferred tourist attraction τ_i. In equation 6.5, $c(\pi_t^*)$ is the expected total cost that a backpacker will spend on running his/her optimal itinerary. $c(\tau_{r,r+1})$ is the cost of moving from the rth tourist attraction to the (r+1)th tourist attraction.

The utility-satisfaction of a backpacker is modeled as Figure 6-2 shows, whereas the cost-satisfaction is modeled as Figure 6-3 shows. Equations 6.6 and 6.7 show the satisfaction of a backpacker which considers both the utility and cost.

$$u(\pi_t^*) = \sum_{i=1}^{n} u(\tau_i) \quad \text{.........(6.4)}$$

$$c(\pi_t^*) = \sum_{r=1}^{n-1} c(\tau_{r,r+1}) \quad \text{.........(6.5)}$$

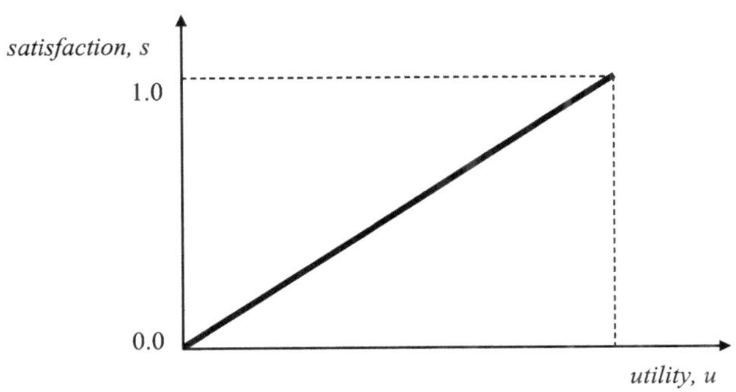

Figure 6-2 Utility-satisfaction relationship of a backpacker

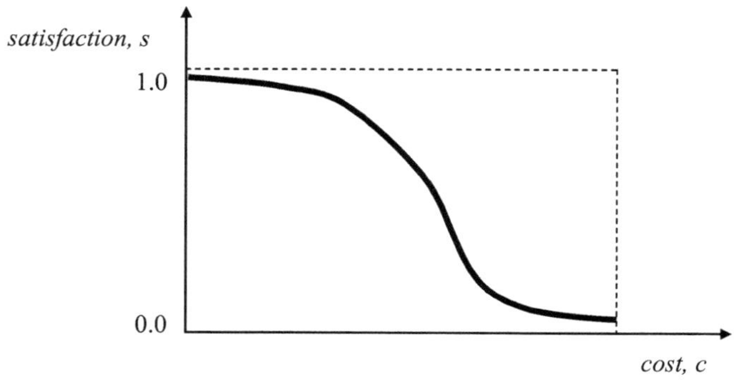

Figure 6-3 Cost-satisfaction relationship of a backpacker

In equation 6.6, the cost part forms a sigmoid model where β is a given positive real number. w_u and w_c are the relative importance of utility and cost. Equation 6.7 shows that the sum of w_u and w_c equals 1.

$$s_t(u,c) = w_u \cdot u + w_c \cdot \left[1.0 - c^{\beta}/(1+c^{\beta})\right], \beta \in R^{+} \quad (6.6)$$

$$w_u + w_c = 1 \quad (6.7)$$

The objectives of the backpackers B1, B2 and B3 as we classify in Section 6.1 are re-modeled as follows.

(1) j^{th} backpacker B1:

Plan

$$\text{mu}_j.\pi^{*} = \{(\tau_r.\text{sp}_m, \tau_{r+1}.\text{sp}_n) \mid \tau_r, \tau_{r+1} \in \text{SP}, 1 \le r \le L-1, m,n,r,L \in \text{N}^{+}\} \quad (6.8)$$

Maximize

$$s_j(u,c)$$

Subject to

$$\text{dist}(\text{mu}_j.\Pi_0, \text{mu}_j.\tau_1.\eta)/\text{mu}_j.\text{v} + \sum_{r=1}^{L} \text{mu}_j.\tau_r.\delta + \sum_{r=1}^{L-1} \kappa_{\tau_r,\tau_{r+1}}.\text{time} \le T \quad (6.9)$$

$$\text{dist}(\text{mu}_j.\Pi_0, \text{mu}_j.\tau_1.\eta)/\text{mu}_j.\text{v} \le \tau_1.\text{s}_m, \quad (6.10)$$

$$\forall r \;\; \tau_{\mathrm{r}}.\mathrm{s}_m + \tau_{\mathrm{r}}.\delta + \kappa_{\tau_r,\tau_{r+1}}.\mathrm{time} \le \tau_{\mathrm{r+1}}.\mathrm{s}_n \quad (6.11)$$

(2) j^{th} backpacker B2 or B3:

Plan

$$\mathrm{mu}_j.\pi_t^{\,*} = \{(\tau_r.\mathrm{sp}_m, \tau_{r+1}.\mathrm{sp}_n) \mid \tau_r, \tau_{r+1} \in \mathrm{SP} - \pi_t^{\,-}, 1 \le r \le K-1, m, n, r, K \in \mathrm{N}^+\} \quad (6.12)$$

$$\mathrm{mu}_j.\pi_t^{\,-} = \{\hat{\tau}_q \mid \hat{\tau}_q \in \mathrm{SP}, \hat{\tau}_q \text{ is visited, } q \in \mathrm{N}^+\} \quad (6.13)$$

Maximize

$$s_{j,t}(u,c)$$

Subject to

$$t + \sum_{r=1}^{K} \mathrm{mu}_j.\tau_r.\delta + \sum_{\mathrm{r}=1}^{K-1} \kappa_{\tau_r,\tau_{r+1}}.\mathrm{time} \le T \quad (6.14)$$

$$t + \mathrm{dist}(\mathrm{mu}_j.\Pi_t, \mathrm{mu}_j.\tau_1.\eta) / \mathrm{mu}_j.\mathrm{v} \le \tau_1.\mathrm{s}_m \quad (6.15)$$

$$\forall r \;\; \tau_{\mathrm{r}}.\mathrm{s}_m + \tau_{\mathrm{r}}.\delta + \kappa_{\tau_r,\tau_{r+1}}.\mathrm{time} \le \tau_{\mathrm{r+1}}.\mathrm{s}_n \quad \text{(same as 6.11)}$$

Chapter 7 Experimental Design

This chapter designs experiments to observe the performance of the SPA+2S-DORA. We organize this chapter as follows. Section 7.1 sets up the experimental environment for the traveling backpacker problem outlined in Chapter 6. Section 7.2 defines the metrics to measure the performance of the SPA+2S-DORA. Section 7.3 designs five experiments.

7.1 Settings

We set up the experimental environment for the traveling backpacker problem as follows:

1. **Time period**: the time period *T* for mobile users to plan their itineraries is set to be 45 unit times, and one unit time is equal to 0.5 hour.
2. **Tourist attractions**: Six tourist attractions, including lighthouse, museum, circus, classic music concert, puppet show and ancient castle, are scattered over the mobile city as shown in Figure 7-1, and their locations are listed in Table 7.1. We set their service timetables as in Table 7.2.

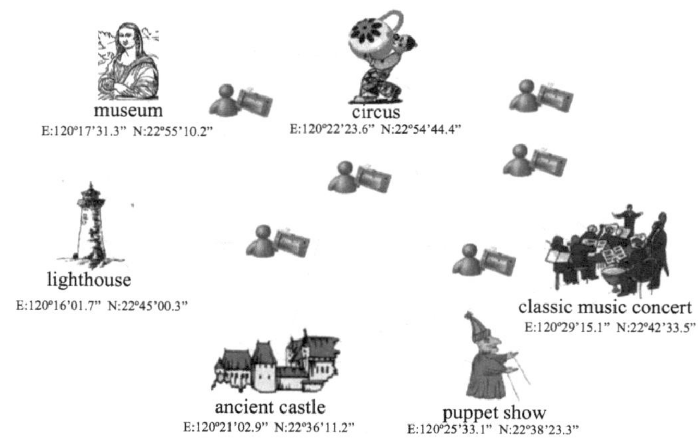

Figure 7-1 Locations of tourist attractions

Table 7.1 Location of the six tourist attractions

Label	Tourist attraction	Location η
sp_1	lighthouse	E:120°16'01.7" N:22°45'00.3"
sp_2	museum	E:120°17'31.3" N:22°55'10.2"
sp_3	circus	E:120°22'23.6" N:22°54'44.4"
sp_4	classic music concert	E:120°29'15.1" N:22°42'33.5"
sp_5	puppet show	E:120°25'33.1" N:22°38'23.3"
sp_6	ancient castle	E:120°21'02.9" N:22°36'11.2"

Table 7.2 Settings of the six tourist attractions

Tourist attraction	Starting time of service cycles **S**	Capacity σ	Cycle time χ
sp_1	1, 10, 17, 26, 33, 43	10	3
sp_2	3, 8, 19, 24, 35, 40	12	4
sp_3	5, 21, 37,41, 45	12	3
sp_4	10, 26, 42	10	4
sp_5	1, 6, 11, 17, 22, 27, 33, 38, 43	10	3
sp_6	2, 8, 18, 24, 34, 40	10	3

Table 7.3 Cost spent while moving between public transportations

	sp_1	sp_2	sp_3	sp_4	sp_5	sp_6
sp_1	0	20	30	30	30	20
sp_2	20	0	10	40	40	40
sp_3	30	10	0	30	40	40
sp_4	30	40	30	0	10	20
sp_5	30	40	40	10	0	10
sp_6	20	40	40	20	10	0

3. **Backpackers**: The number of backpackers is different from busy and slack travel seasons. In a busy season, 100 backpackers visit the tourist attractions, whereas in a slack season, 30 backpackers visit the tourist attractions. A backpacker is initially positioned by randomly generating his/her longitude value in the range from 120.2°E to 120.5°E and latitude from 22.6°N to 23°N. A backpacker's individual preferences are generated by randomly picking up 3 to 6 tourist attractions and randomly ranking them. A backpacker's moving velocity is 10 km per unit time. The importance levels of a backpacker's utility w_u and cost w_c are 0.6 and 0.4, respectively. β is 1.0.
4. **Cost and time required to move among public transportation**: Tables 7.3 and 7.4 respectively show the cost and time spent for a backpacker to move from one tourist attraction to another.
5. **Size of a coordination network**: In order to ensure that every round of coordination can be completed in a short time, the maximum layers of a coordination network is set to 3, and a node in the network has at most 3 child nodes. w of the BEB is 5 sec.

Table 7.4 Time spent while moving between public transportations

	sp_1	sp_2	sp_3	sp_4	sp_5	sp_6
sp_1	0	2	3	3	3	2
sp_2	2	0	1	4	4	4
sp_3	3	1	0	3	4	4
sp_4	3	4	3	0	1	2
sp_5	3	4	4	1	0	1
sp_6	2	4	4	2	1	0

7.2 Metrics to Measure Performance

A traveling backpacker's objective is to gain his or her maximal satisfaction on his or her itinerary. The tourist attractions on the other hand will benefit if their capacity utilization rates are uplifted. We thus define two metrics to test the significance of the performance improvement made by the SPA+2S-DORA. These two metrics are: (1) **satisfaction** of a traveling backpacker after s/he completes his/her itinerary, and (2) the **capacity utilization rate** of a tourist attraction.

The satisfaction of traveling backpacker mu_j is in equations 6.4 to 6.7. The capacity utilization rate $sp_i.cur_p$ of the pth service cycle of the ith tourist attraction sp_i is in equation 7.1. The maximum $sp_i.cur_p$ is 1.0. If $sp_i.cur_p=1.0$, the pth cycle's capacity of the ith attraction is fully utilized. If the $sp_i.cur_p<1.0$, it is underutilized. If $sp_i.cur_p>1.0$, it is over demanded, and it is not able to serve all backpackers. These two metrics will be used to compare the experimental results and test the significance of the differences between the results.

$$sp_i.cur_p = \frac{\sum_{j=1}^{N} sp_i.\varphi_{p,j}}{sp_i.\chi} \qquad (7.1)$$

7.3 Experimental Design

We conduct five experiments. The first experiment evaluates the significance of improvement made by SPA+2S-DORA on mobile users' joint itineraries. The second experiment compares B3's satisfactions in a distributed and a centralized environment. The third experiment investigates the influences of two parameters - the ratio of B3 and the reservation percentages reserved for locale backpackers. The fourth experiment investigates the B3's satisfaction improvements when they perceive a context variation. The last experiment investigates how the B3 adjust their itineraries when they encounter an exception.

These five experiments are portrayed as follows. The experimental environment is built in a simulated agent system.

Experiment 1

In the first experiment, backpackers B1, B2 and B3 are respectively put into the busy travel season scenario under the same experimental settings. We carry out this experiment 10 rounds to evaluate the SPA+2S-DORA under 10 pre-generated experimental settings. In this experiment, we evaluate the satisfactions of backpackers and the utilization rates of service providers.

Experiment 2

The second experiment makes a comparison on the application of the SPA+2S-DORA in a distributed environment and a centralized environment. This experiment is executed only at t=0 under the same experimental settings in Experiment 1. In the distributed environment, all backpackers individually plan their itineraries. All backpackers are allowed to improve their itineraries at most 5 times if they have better itineraries. On the other in the centralized environment, all backpackers' itineraries are sequentially planned and then are orderly improved until the environment is in a stable state, *i.e.*, their itineraries cannot be further improved.

Experiment 3

The third experiment investigates the influences of two parameters ρ and θ on the backpackers B3 and B1 and on the tourist attractions, where ρ is the ratio of B3 and θ the percentage of tickets that tourist attractions reserve for locale backpackers. The backpackers B3, though making reservations before their travels, will compete with backpackers B1 to get the locale tickets due to the limited online reservations. In this experiment, we assume that the θs of all sp_i are identical. Table 7.5 lists the value combination of the variables (ρ,θ). We build two different environments - the first one is a busy season, and the second a slack season. We conduct the experiments only at t=0 based on the value combinations in busy and slack seasons.

Table 7.5 Value combinations of (ρ,θ)

(0.2, 20%)	(0.2, 40%)	(0.2, 60%)	(0.2, 80%)
(0.4, 20%)	(0.4, 40%)	(0.4, 60%)	(0.4, 80%)
(0.6, 20%)	(0.6, 40%)	(0.6, 60%)	(0.6, 80%)
(0.8, 20%)	(0.8, 40%)	(0.8, 60%)	(0.8, 80%)

Experiment 4

The fourth experiment simulates a context variation in a busy travel season where at *t*=30, a thunderstorm suddenly occurs, and the weather report says that the storm will end after *t*=35. The backpackers B3 who have booked the tickets to the lighthouse (sp_1) and plan to enjoy sp_1's service during that period will cancel the reservation and modify their itineraries. The context variation immediately reduces the B3's expected satisfaction with their schedules. This experiment uses the first round setting of the first experiment to investigate the advantages of applying SPA+2S-DORA to improve backpackers' joint itineraries.

Experiment 5

The fifth experiment simulates an exception in a busy travel season. The exception is that at *t*=20, a heavy traffic jam occurs on the road that connects the museum and the circus, and later at *t*=35, the road is clear. The backpackers, who follow their itineraries to move from the museum to the circus during that period, will change their itineraries. This experiment uses the first round setting of the first experiment to investigate the advantages of applying SPA+2S-DORA to improve backpackers' joint itineraries.

The next chapter presents the results from the above-mentioned five experiments.

Chapter 8 Experimental Results and Discussions

In this chapter, Section 8.1 shows the experimental results, and Section 8.2 discusses the experimental results.

8.1 Experimental Results

Results of Experiment 1

Tables 8.1 and 8.2 show the experimental results from the first round of the first experiment. Table 8.1 lists the satisfactions of backpackers B1, B2 and B3. Table 8.2 lists the capacity utilization conditions of the service providers corresponding to B1, B2 and B3. Table 8.3 presents the effectiveness of the SPA+2S-DORA by making comparisons on backpackers' actual satisfaction and on the service providers' utilization in ten rounds of experiments.

In table 8.1, column B0 shows all backpackers' expected satisfaction when they consider only temporal constraint, and ignore the capacity constraints of tourist attractions. Columns B1, B2 and B3 demonstrate the satisfactions of backpackers B1, B2 and B3. In Table 8.1, a backpacker's satisfaction value, marked with grey background color, is those backpackers whose satisfaction values are not identical in the four columns.

Table 8.1 Backpackers' satisfaction obtained in the first round experiment

#	**B0**	B1	B2	B3
1	**0.37**	0.37	0.37	0.37
2	**0.31**	0.31	0.31	0.31
3	**0.31**	0.31	0.31	0.31
4	**0.32**	0.32	0.32	0.32
5	**0.31**	0.31	0.31	0.31
6	**0.43**	0.43	0.43	0.43
7	**0.31**	0.31	0.31	0.31
8	**0.31**	0.31	0.31	0.31
9	**0.31**	0.31	0.31	0.31

#	**B0**	B1	B2	B3
10	**0.41**	0.41	0.41	0.41
11	**0.31**	0.31	0.31	0.31
12	**0.31**	0.31	0.31	0.31
13	**0.37**	0.37	0.37	0.37
14	**0.37**	0.37	0.37	0.37
15	**0.43**	0.43	0.43	0.43
16	**0.37**	0.37	0.37	0.37
17	**0.43**	0.43	0.43	0.43
18	**0.37**	0.37	0.37	0.37

#	**B0**	B1	B2	B3
19	**0.41**	0.41	0.41	0.41
20	**0.37**	0.37	0.37	0.37
21	**0.37**	0.37	0.37	0.37
22	**0.37**	0.37	0.37	0.37
23	**0.41**	0.41	0.41	0.41
24	**0.37**	0.37	0.37	0.37
25	**0.31**	0.31	0.31	0.31
26	**0.31**	0.31	0.31	0.31
27	**0.31**	0.31	0.31	0.31
28	**0.37**	0.37	0.37	0.37
29	**0.37**	0.37	0.37	0.37
30	**0.41**	0.41	0.41	0.41
31	**0.41**	0.41	0.41	0.41
32	**0.40**	0.40	0.40	0.40
33	**0.31**	0.31	0.31	0.31
34	**0.43**	0.43	0.43	0.43
35	**0.31**	0.31	0.31	0.31
36	**0.37**	0.37	0.37	0.37
37	**0.31**	0.21	0.31	0.31
38	**0.40**	0.40	0.40	0.40
39	**0.41**	0.41	0.41	0.41
40	**0.31**	0.12	0.31	0.31
41	**0.41**	0.41	0.29	0.29
42	**0.41**	0.41	0.41	0.41
43	**0.33**	0.33	0.33	0.33
44	**0.41**	0.37	0.37	0.37
45	**0.43**	0.32	0.38	0.38
46	**0.37**	0.37	0.37	0.37
47	**0.41**	0.41	0.41	0.41
48	**0.41**	0.37	0.37	0.37
49	**0.31**	0.31	0.31	0.31
50	**0.41**	0.41	0.41	0.41
51	**0.43**	0.30	0.38	0.38
52	**0.31**	0.31	0.31	0.31
53	**0.31**	0.24	0.31	0.31
54	**0.37**	0.31	0.37	0.37
55	**0.37**	0.19	0.19	0.19
56	**0.32**	0.14	0.13	0.13

#	**B0**	B1	B2	B3
57	**0.43**	0.29	0.29	0.36
58	**0.43**	0.29	0.29	0.29
59	**0.31**	0.21	0.13	0.13
60	**0.43**	0.32	0.32	0.40
61	**0.43**	0.38	0.38	0.38
62	**0.41**	0.37	0.37	0.37
63	**0.37**	0.20	0.37	0.37
64	**0.43**	0.41	0.41	0.41
65	**0.37**	0.31	0.19	0.19
66	**0.31**	0.31	0.31	0.31
67	**0.31**	0.22	0.21	0.31
68	**0.41**	0.29	0.37	0.37
69	**0.31**	0.24	0.31	0.31
70	**0.37**	0.19	0.31	0.31
71	**0.37**	0.31	0.31	0.31
72	**0.43**	0.32	0.32	0.35
73	**0.43**	0.21	0.32	0.32
74	**0.41**	0.33	0.33	0.33
75	**0.33**	0.33	0.33	0.33
76	**0.37**	0.16	0.32	0.32
77	**0.31**	0.21	0.31	0.31
78	**0.31**	0.31	0.31	0.31
79	**0.37**	0.37	0.37	0.37
80	**0.31**	0.31	0.31	0.31
81	**0.31**	0.24	0.31	0.31
82	**0.43**	0.41	0.40	0.40
83	**0.31**	0.21	0.31	0.31
84	**0.43**	0.38	0.43	0.43
85	**0.31**	0.11	0.31	0.31
86	**0.31**	0.31	0.31	0.31
87	**0.41**	0.37	0.37	0.40
88	**0.41**	0.21	0.33	0.33
89	**0.41**	0.17	0.25	0.25
90	**0.41**	0.13	0.37	0.40
91	**0.37**	0.19	0.31	0.37
92	**0.31**	0.24	0.31	0.31
93	**0.33**	0.14	0.33	0.33
94	**0.37**	0.19	0.16	0.16

#	**B0**	B1	B2	B3
95	**0.31**	0.12	0.11	0.31
96	**0.41**	0.33	0.29	0.32
97	**0.31**	0.21	0.21	0.30

#	**B0**	B1	B2	B3
98	**0.41**	0.37	0.37	0.40
99	**0.43**	0.26	0.21	0.29
100	**0.41**	0.37	0.29	0.29

B0: Backpacker considers the temporal constraints only   B1: Backpacker without any devices

B2: Backpacker with a pure mobile device   B3: Backpacker with the SPA+2S-DORA

Table 8.2 shows the capacity utilization rate of every service provider's service cycle corresponding to backpackers B1(a), B2(b) and B3(c) respectively. For example, in the sp_1 row of Table 8.2(a), 0.9 means that the sp_1's first cycle is 90% utilized; 2.30 means that the second cycle of sp_1 is over-demanded by 130%. The over-demanded part will not be fulfilled. In Table 8.2(a), the over-demanded cycles are marked with boldface number.

Table 8.2 Capacity utilization rates ($sp_i.cur_p$) of service providers

(a) Corresponding to backpacker B1

Tourist attraction	Capacity utilization rate of service cycle $sp_i.cur_p$
sp_1	0.90, **2.30**, **1.70**, 0.60, 0.30, 0.00
sp_2	**1.58**, 0.25, 0.58, 0.42, 1.00, 0.08
sp_3	**1.25**, **1.33**, 0.83, 0.50, 0.00
sp_4	**3.00**, **2.00**, 0.00
sp_5	0.60, **1.60**, 0.20, **1.80**, 0.70, 0.10, 0.70, 0.00, 0.00
sp_6	**1.50**, 0.90, **2.20**, 0.60, 0.20, 0.20

(b) Corresponding to backpacker B2

Tourist attraction	Capacity utilization rate of service cycle $sp_i.cur_p$
sp_1	1.00, 1.00, 1.00, 1.00, 1.00, 0.00
sp_2	1.00, 1.00, 1.00, 0.17, 0.42, 0.33
sp_3	1.00, 1.00, 1.00, 0.83, 0.00
sp_4	1.00, 1.00, 0.00
sp_5	0.90, 1.00, 1.00, 1.00, 0.60, 0.00, 0.90, 0.30, 0.00
sp_6	1.00, 1.00, 1.00, 1.00, 1.00, 0.40

(c) Corresponding to backpacker B3

Tourist attraction	Capacity utilization rate of service cycle $sp_i.cur_p$
sp_1	1.00, 1.00, 1.00, 1.00, 0.90, 0.40
sp_2	1.00, 0.92, 0.83, 0.17, 0.67, 0.50
sp_3	1.00, 0.75, 1.00, 1.00, 0.17
sp_4	1.00, 1.00, 0.90
sp_5	0.90, 1.00, 0.90, 1.00, 0.60, 0.10, 0.90, 0.20, 0.20
sp_6	0.90, 1.00, 1.00, 1.00, 1.00, 0.40

Table 8.3 shows the comparisons made on the satisfaction of backpackers and on the average utilization rates of their corresponding service providers for ten rounds. In Table 8.3, all of the over-demanded utilization rates are truncated to 1.0 before making comparisons. We evaluate the significance using pairwise *t*-test.

Table 8.3 Comparisons on backpackers' satisfactions and service providers' utilization rates

Round #	Satisfaction, *s*		Capacity utilization rate, cur	
	$s_{B3}>s_{B1}$	$s_{B3}>s_{B2}$	$cur_{B3}>cur_{B1}$	$cur_{B3}>cur_{B2}$
1	$1.22x10^{-5}$**	0.002**	0.003**	0.117
2	$5.11x10^{-7}$**	0.001**	0.000**	0.050*
3	$3.74x10^{-7}$**	0.006**	0.000**	0.035*
4	$2.16x10^{-6}$**	0.027*	0.004**	0.024*
5	$5.07x10^{-5}$**	0.001**	0.001**	0.050*
6	$6.85x10^{-8}$**	0.000**	0.008**	0.121
7	$1.54x10^{-7}$**	0.020*	0.005**	0.169
8	$2.58x10^{-6}$**	0.000**	0.005**	0.100
9	$4.51x10^{-4}$**	0.013*	0.002**	0.122
10	0.001**	0.003**	0.003**	0.070

Significance level: *<0.05 **<0.01

Results of Experiment 2

Table 8.4 presents the comparison results of Experiment 2. The comparison is evaluated using pairwise t-test. The comparison reveals that backpackers' satisfactions have no significant difference whether they are in a distributed or a centralized computing environment, except for the result from the second round experiment.

Table 8.4 Comparisons on applying 2S-DORA in a centralized and in a distributed environment

Round #	Satisfaction, s
	$s_{centralized} > s_{distributed}$
1	0.313
2	0.011*
3	0.340
4	0.110
5	0.242
6	0.033
7	0.064
8	0.354
9	0.457
10	0.344

Significance level: *<0.05 **<0.01

Results of Experiment 3

Table 8.5 demonstrates the results of Experiment 3. Table 8.5(a) shows the backpackers' average satisfaction under the first round's setting of the first experiment in a busy travel season. Table 8.5(b) shows the backpackers' average satisfaction in a slack travel season. Table 8.5 presents B3's average **initial expected**, average **improved expected**, and average **actual** satisfactions. The actual satisfaction is a backpacker's perceived satisfaction after s/he has fulfilled his/her itinerary. B3's actual satisfaction can be larger than their expected because B3 will compete with B1 to get the locale tickets. Table 8.5 also presents B1's average initial expected satisfaction and average actual satisfaction. B1 only buys locale tickets. They do not make any reservation before their travels. B1's actual satisfaction can be less than their expected because B1 is very likely to get no locale ticket.

Table 8.5 Average satisfaction of B3 and B1 with different (ρ,θ) combination

(a) In a busy travel season

Exp#	Type	Ratio (ρ) (Amount)	Satisfaction	locale reservation percentage(θ)			
				20%	40%	60%	80%
1	B3	0.2 (20)	initial expected	0.362	0.351	0.364	0.290
			improved expected	0.362	0.351	0.370	0.304
			actual	0.362	0.351	0.370	0.315
	B1	(80)	initial expected	0.367	0.370	0.364	0.371
			improved expected	-	-	-	-
			actual	0.237	0.246	0.252	0.272
2	B3	0.4 (40)	initial expected	0.360	0.350	0.339	0.195
			improved expected	0.365	0.355	0.350	0.204
			actual	0.365	0.355	0.351	0.303
	B1	(60)	initial expected	0.366	0.371	0.367	0.363
			improved expected	-	-	-	-
			actual	0.212	0.224	0.262	0.258
3	B3	0.6 (60)	initial expected	0.336	0.342	0.269	0.152
			improved expected	0.352	0.350	0.293	0.159
			actual	0.356	0.354	0.312	0.263
	B1	(40)	initial expected	0.372	0.369	0.366	0.376
			improved expected	-	-	-	-
			actual	0.209	0.217	0.269	0.297
4	B3	0.8 (80)	initial expected	0.324	0.319	0.197	0.103
			improved expected	0.337	0.328	0.204	0.113
			actual	0.340	0.342	0.311	0.280
	B1	(20)	initial expected	0.378	0.381	0.363	0.360
			improved expected	-	-	-	-
			actual	0.258	0.278	0.288	0.286

(b) In a slack travel season

Exp#	Type	Ratio (ρ) (Amount)	Satisfaction	locale reservation percentage (θ)			
				20%	40%	60%	80%
1	B3	0.2 (6)	initial expected	0.385	0.358	0.357	0.365
			improved expected	0.385	0.358	0.357	0.365
			actual	0.385	0.358	0.357	0.365
	B1	(24)	initial expected	0.349	0.356	0.356	0.354
			improved expected	-	-	-	-
			actual	0.349	0.356	0.356	0.354
2	B3	0.4 (12)	initial expected	0.351	0.353	0.337	0.338
			improved expected	0.351	0.353	0.337	0.349
			actual	0.351	0.353	0.337	0.349
	B1	(18)	initial expected	0.360	0.358	0.369	0.353
			improved expected	-	-	-	-
			real	0.360	0.358	0.369	0.353
3	B3	0.6 (18)	initial expected	0.359	0.354	0.358	0.301
			improved expected	0.359	0.354	0.358	0.319
			actual	0.359	0.354	0.358	0.349
	B1	(12)	initial expected	0.352	0.360	0.354	0.366
			improved expected	-	-	-	-
			actual	0.352	0.360	0.354	0.366
4	B3	0.8 (24)	initial expected	0.349	0.350	0.350	0.291
			improved expected	0.349	0.350	0.350	0.311
			actual	0.349	0.350	0.355	0.348
	B1	(6)	initial expected	0.384	0.382	0.352	0.372
			improved expected	-	-	-	-
			actual	0.384	0.382	0.352	0.372

To make the satisfaction differences of B1 and B3 clearly observed, we translate the data of Table 8.5(a) and (b) respectively into Figures 8.1 and 8.2. Figure 8.1(a) demonstrates the variation of B3's initial expected, improved expected and actual satisfaction under different (ρ, θ) combinations in a busy season. Figure 8.1(b) demonstrates B1's initial expected and actual satisfaction in a busy season. Figure 8.1(c) makes a comparison on B1's and B3's actual satisfaction. Figure 8.2 demonstrates the similar comparisons in a slack season as what Figure 8.1 does.

To evaluate the improvement effect made by 2S-DORA, Table 8.6 makes comparisons on backpackers B3's average initial and average improved expected satisfactions. Tables 8.6(a) and 8.6(b) respectively evaluate the improvement in a busy and a slack travel season, where the statistical data represents the percentages and significance of the improvements. For instance, if ρ=0.2 and θ=80% in the rush travel reason, the statistical data 4.83% (0.101) indicates that the improvement percentage is 4.83% and the significance level is 0.101. The improvement percentage = (improved - initial) / initial. The significance is evaluated using pairwise *t*-test.

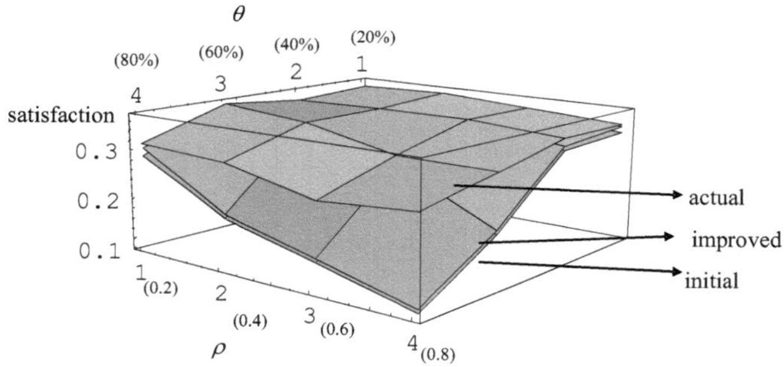

(a) Comparison on B3's satisfaction

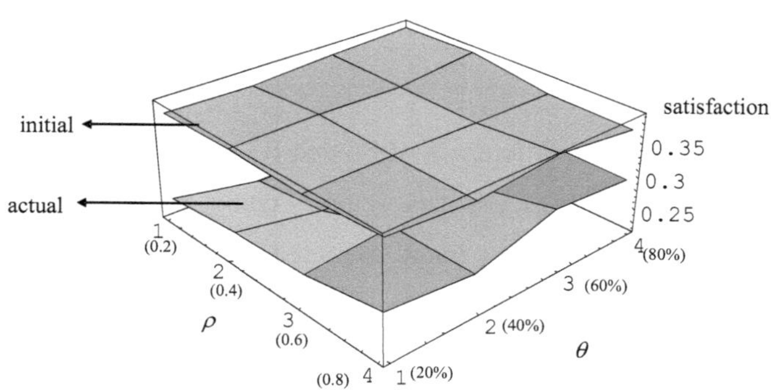

(b) Comparison on B1's satisfaction

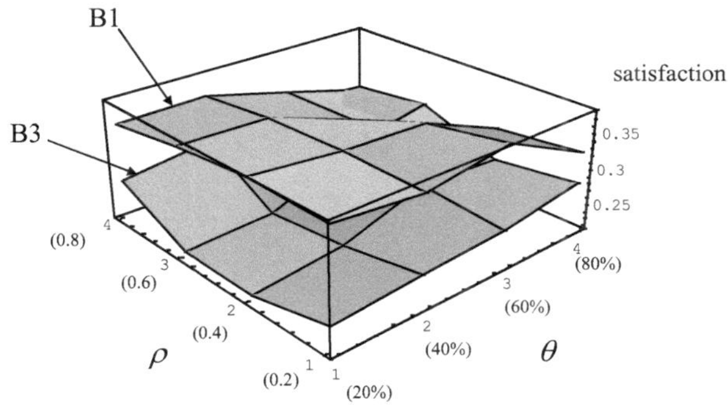

(c) Comparison on B1 and B3's actual satisfactions

Figure 8-1 Variation of B1 and B3's satisfactions in a busy season

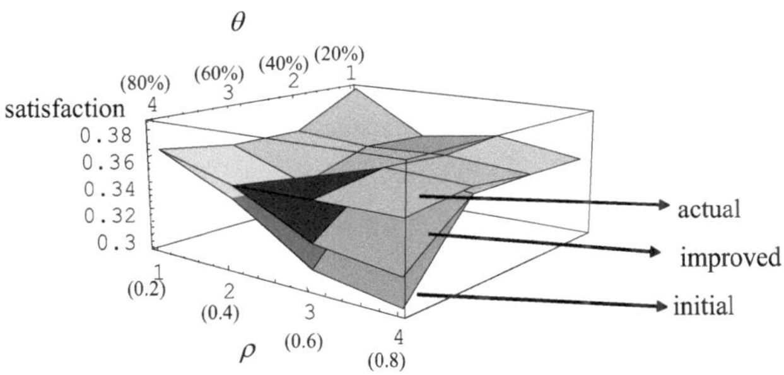

(a) Comparison on B3's satisfaction

(b)

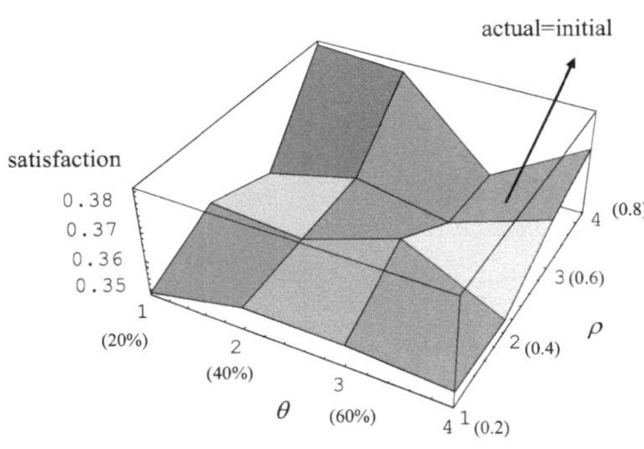

(b) Comparison on B1's satisfaction

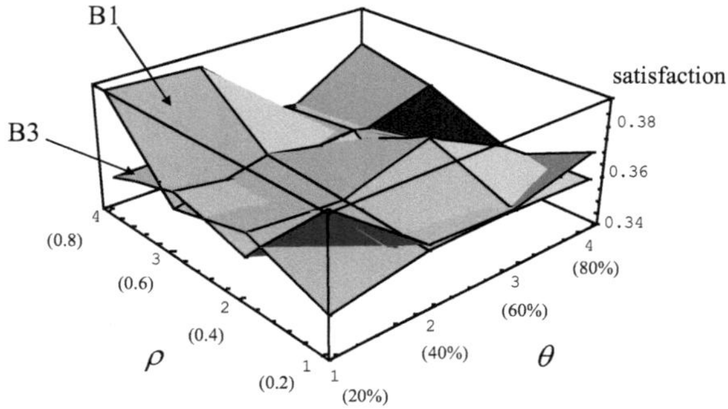

(c) Comparison on B1 and B3's actual satisfaction

Figure 8-2 Variation of B1 and B3's satisfactions in a slack season

Table 8.6 2S-DORA improvement effect under different (ρ,θ) combination

(a) In a busy travel season

ρ \ θ	20%	40%	60%	80%
0.2	0.00% (-)	0.00% (0.165)	1.65% (0.046*)	4.83% (0.101)
0.4	1.39% (0.029*)	1.43% (0.047**)	3.24% (0.018*)	4.62% (0.055)
0.6	4.76% (0.004**)	2.34% (0.021*)	8.92% (0.001**)	4.61% (0.009**)
0.8	4.01% (0.001**)	2.82% (0.003**)	3.55% (0.034*)	9.71% (0.008**)

(b) In a slack travel season

ρ \ θ	20%	40%	60%	80%
0.2	0.00% (-)	0.00% (-)	0.00% (-)	0.00% (-)
0.4	0.00% (-)	0.00% (-)	0.00% (-)	3.25% (0.101)
0.6	0.00% (-)	0.00% (-)	0.00% (-)	5.98% (0.083)
0.8	0.00% (-)	0.00% (-)	0.00% (-)	6.87% (0.015*)

Additionally, Table 8.7 makes comparisons on B1 and B3's actual satisfactions. Table 8.7 reveals that B3's actual satisfaction is generally higher than B1's. Tables 8.7(a) and 8.7(b) show the comparisons in a busy and a slack travel season. The comparisons are carried out using *t*-test.

Table 8.7 Actual satisfaction comparison between B1 and B3

(a) In a busy season

Ratio(ρ)	Comparison	locale reservation percentage(θ)			
		20%	40%	60%	80%
0.2	$S_{B3,actual} > S_{B1,\ actual}$	$4.17x10^{-10}$**	$1.65x10^{-8}$**	$1.84x10^{-10}$**	0.028*
0.4		$1.57x10^{-12}$**	$2.77x10^{-11}$**	$2.79x10^{-7}$**	0.038*
0.6		$3.97\ x10^{-9}$**	$5.81x10^{-8}$**	0.005**	0.242
0.8		0.002**	0.003**	0.161	0.412

Significance level: *<0.05 **<0.01

(b) In a slack season

Ratio(ρ)	Comparison	locale reservation percentage(θ)			
		20%	40%	60%	80%
0.2	$S_{B3,actual} > S_{B1,\ actual}$	0.067	0.465	0.484	0.321
0.4		0.289	0.392	0.019*	0.411
0.6		0.301	0.340	0.407	0.166
0.8		0.102	0.074	0.446	0.161

Significance level: *<0.05 **<0.01

Results of Experiment 4

Table 8.8 lists the backpackers B3 whose itineraries and expected satisfaction change around the time that they perceive the context variation. In this table, Column 1 denotes the backpackers' numbers. Columns 2 and 3 show the backpackers' itineraries and their expected satisfaction before the context variation respectively. An itinerary is a backpacker's travel schedule that contains a sequence of tourist attractions and the number of their service cycle that s/he is going to visit. For example, the backpacker #3's itinerary classic[1]lighthouse[3] means that s/he will visit the classic music concert to enjoy its first service cycle, and then go to the lighthouse to enjoy its third cycle. Column 4, entitled ‘CV’, shows the backpackers’ expected satisfaction after the context variation. Backpackers, whose expected satisfaction marked with the dark gray background color, are those who impacted by the context variation. Their expected satisfactions are significantly reduced. In column 4, the other backpackers are those who benefits from the context variation to improve their itineraries. Columns 5 and 6 are the backpackers’ improved itineraries and expected satisfactions. Column 6 reveals that some of the backpackers’ expected satisfactions are recovered or increased, and the others’ expected satisfactions remain reduced. The improvement made by the SPA+2S-DORA is highly significant with p-value=0.004.

Table 8.8 Variation of B3’ itineraries and satisfactions due to a context variation

#	Before the context		CV	Impacted by the context and improved by SPA+2S-DORA	
	Itinerary	*ES*	*ES*	Itinerary	*ES*
3	classic[1]lighthouse[3]	0.31	**0.21**	classic[1]circus[2]lighthouse[6]	0.31
6	classic[1]castle[3]lighthouse[4]museum[5]circus[4]	0.43	**0.35**	classic[1]castle[3]museum[5]circus[4]	0.35
9	lighthouse[4]puppet[9]	0.31	**0.22**	museum[4]puppet[7]lighthouse[6]	0.30
10	classic[1]lighthouse[3]museum[4]circus[3]	0.41	**0.23**	classic[1]circus[3]museum[6]	0.29
12	puppet[2]lighthouse[3]	0.31	**0.22**	puppet[2]	0.22
14	classic[1]castle[3]lighthouse[4]	0.37	**0.19**	classic[1]castle[3]	0.19
26	circus[1]lighthouse[3]	0.31	**0.26**	circus[1]	0.26
32	puppet[2]classic[1]lighthouse[3]museum[4]	0.40	**0.25**	puppet[2]classic[1]museum[4]	0.25
39	circus[1]lighthouse[3]castle[4]puppet[7]	0.41	**0.35**	circus[1]museum[3]puppet[6]lighthouse[6]	0.32
41	puppet[2]classic[3]	0.29	**0.29**	puppet[2]castle[4]classic[3]	0.37
45	museum[2]lighthouse[3]castle[4]puppet[7]	0.38	**0.32**	museum[2]puppet[4]castle[4]lighthouse[6]	0.38
46	circus[1]lighthouse[3]castle[4]	0.37	**0.31**	circus[1]castle[4]	0.31
50	circus[1]museum[3]lighthouse[4]castle[5]	0.41	**0.29**	circus[1]museum[3]castle[5]	0.29
51	museum[1]lighthouse[3]castle[4]puppet[7]	0.38	**0.29**	museum[1]castle[4]puppet[7]	0.29
53	museum[3]lighthouse[4]	0.31	**0.24**	museum[3]	0.24
54	castle[1]lighthouse[4]circus[3]	0.37	**0.31**	castle[1]circus[3]	0.31
55	castle[2]museum[3]	0.19	**0.19**	castle[2]classic[3]	0.25
64	puppet[1]castle[2]lighthouse[4]circus[3]	0.41	**0.35**	puppet[1]castle[2]circus[3]	0.35
66	circus[1]lighthouse[4]	0.31	**0.24**	circus[1]	0.24
76	puppet[1]castle[2]	0.32	**0.32**	puppet[1]castle[2]classic[3]	0.37
84	puppet[1]castle[4]lighthouse[4]museum[5]circus[4]	0.43	**0.38**	puppet[1]castle[4]museum[5]circus[4]	0.38

#	Before the context		CV	Impacted by the context and improved by SPA+2S-DORA	
	Itinerary	*ES*	*ES*	Itinerary	*ES*
85	circus[1]lighthouse[3]museum[4]	0.31	**0.21**	circus[1]	0.24
87	museum[2]castle[4]lighthouse[4]puppet[7]circus[4]	0.40	**0.36**	museum[2]castle[4]puppet[7]circus[4]	0.36
88	castle[1]puppet[5]circus[4]	0.33	**0.33**	castle[1]puppet[3]classic[3]	0.38

CV: context variation

Results of Experiment 5

Table 8.9 shows the variations of backpackers' satisfaction in Experiment 5, which are incurred by an exception. Table 8.9 lists the backpackers whose itineraries and expected satisfactions changes around the time the exception happens. Except column 4, the others are the same as those in Table 8.8. Column 4, entitled 'Exception', reveals the backpackers' expected satisfactions after the exception happens. The improvement made by the SPA+2S-DORA is significant with p-value=0.041.

Table 8.9 Variation of B3's itineraries and satisfaction due to an exception

#	Before the context variation		Exception	Impacted by the context and improved by SPA+2S-DORA	
	Itinerary	*ES*	*ES*	Itinerary	*ES*
6	classic[1]castle[3]puppet[4]museum[5]circus[4]	0.43	**0.32**	classic[1]castle[3]puppet[4]museum[5]	0.32
55	castle[2]museum[6]	0.19	**0.19**	castle[2]classic[3]	0.25
60	classic[1]lighthouse[4]museum[6]circus[5]	0.40	**0.35**	classic[1]lighthouse[4]museum[6]	0.35
84	puppet[2]castle[3]lighthouse[6]museum[6]circus[5]	0.43	**0.35**	puppet[2]castle[3]lighthouse[6]museum[6]	0.35
94	circus[4]	0.16	**0.16**	puppet[4]lighthouse[7]circus[4]	0.30
98	lighthouse[5]museum[5]circus[4]	0.37	**0.21**	museum[4]lighthouse[7]castle[6]	0.25

8.2 Discussions

This section discusses the experimental results as follows.

Experiment 1

Tables 8.1 and 8.3 show that if all backpackers are traveling with SPA+2S-DORA embedded mobile device (B3), they will gain higher satisfaction than if they are without any communication device (B1). The difference between these two types of backpackers is highly significant. Namely, in a busy travel season, a backpacker may result in poor itinerary with low satisfaction if s/he does not make reservations beforehand from tourist attractions.

Plus, Table 8.3 demonstrates that B3's satisfaction is higher than B2's. This result is supported by the ten experimental rounds where 70% of them are highly significant and 30% significant. The result highlights the main effects generated by the SPA+2S-DORA.

Table 8.3 further shows that B3 than B1 contributes more to tourist attractions in terms of increasing their utilization rates. This result is supported by 100% of the ten experimental rounds in highly significant level. Table 8.3 also reveals that 40% of the experiments support the result that B3 contributes more than B1 does to increasing the utilization rates of tourist attractions.

This experiment tells that SPA+2S-DORA can help backpackers improve their itineraries by resolving conflicts, which in turn enables backpackers to enjoy more tourist attractions to increase the utilization rates of tourist attractions and prevent the unbalance of their capacity utilization.

Discussing Experiment 2

Table 8.4 shows that though the quality of B3's joint itineraries obtained in the distributed environment is slightly poorer than that obtained in the centralized environment, 90% of the ten experimental rounds show that there exist no significant differences between both results.

This experiment tells that the SPA+2S-DORA, in the distributed environment, perform as well as that in the centralized environment. This experiment proves that 2S-DORA can generate comparatively good itineraries through distributed communication and coordination.

This experiment reveals an additional fact that the termination condition, *e.g.* achieving stability with no possible improvement, of applying the 2S-DORA in a centralized environment can be easily detected. Oppositely, in a distributed environment, for 2S-DORA, the termination condition is not easily detected. Such a situation may result in lots of useless communications and waste the communication resources. To avoid the useless communications and the endless ineffective improvement, the frequency of users' requests must be restricted. A new mechanism, such as a fee charging system, is recommended to the mobile environment.

Discussing Experiment 3

Table 8.5(a), Table 8.6(a) and Figure 8.1(a) show that in a busy travel season, the higher the locale percentage, the more SPA+2S-DORA is needed. Besides, the more the SPA+2S-DORA users, the more possibility that they can improve their itineraries to gain higher expected satisfactions. In Figure 8.1(a), B3's actual satisfaction is higher than their expectation because B3 can compete with B1 to get additional services.

Table 8.5(a) and Figure 8.1(b) reveal that in a busy travel season, B1 will end up with lower actual satisfaction compared with their expectation because B1 buy only locale tickets. They must take the risk of failing to enjoy their desired services.

Table 8.5(a) and Figure 8.1(c) show that B3 obtains higher actual satisfaction than B1 does in a busy travel season, especially when the locale reservation percentage (θ) is low and the ratio (ρ) of B3 is high. Table 8.7(a) further proves the inference. Table 8.7(a) reveals another fact that if ρ and θ are large, B3 will gain less significant advantage than B1. Consequently, backpackers will lack the motivation to use the SPA+2S-DORA.

Table 8.5(b), Table 8.6(b) and Figure 8.2(a) show that in a slack travel season, the SPA+2S-DORA contributes more to B3's average expected satisfaction if ρ and θ are large. Besides, B3 in average will end up more satisfied than expected.

Figure 8.2(b) and Table 8.5(b) show that in a slack travel season, B1 gains satisfaction as they expected. In Figure 8.2(c) and Table 8.7(b), the satisfaction plot and the statistical data shows that in a slack travel season, B3 gains an insignificant advantage over B1.

Discussing Experiment 4 results

Table 8.8 shows that once a context varies, backpackers will first try to adjust their itineraries and then improve the itineraries by making new reservations or exchange their reservations with others. A contextual change may lead the mobile environment to an unstable state. In an unstable state, backpackers are likely to have opportunities to improve their itineraries to make the environment reach another stable state. This experiment reveals that the SPA+2S-DORA can significantly help backpackers improve their itineraries to mitigate the impacts from the context variations.

Discussing Experiment 5

The results of this experiment reveal almost the same outcome as that of experiment 4. That is, backpackers with mobile devices embedded with SPA+2S-DORA have similar responses to the exceptions and context variations. They may cancel the affected reservations, book new capacities or exchange reservations with others to improve their own affected itineraries.

Limitations

There are two major limitations that should be noted. First, a mobile user runs his/her exchange reservation schemes to form a coordination network by sequentially sending `REQUEST` messages to his/her lower-layer users in a unicast mode. The unicast mode than the other modes, such as the multicast mode or the broadcast mode, allows more mobile users to initialize their coordination networks. Nevertheless, the unicast mode than the other modes is likely to spend more time to form an effective coordination network. We do not evaluate the performance of 2S-DORA in different `REQUEST` message sending modes.

Second, we carry out our experiments in a simulated environment because it is very difficult to conduct large-scale experiments in a physical mobile environment. We build a simulated environment in an ordinary PC. The mobile users and the service providers are implemented in the simulated distributed environment. Though we try to make the simulated environment as real as possible, there still exist gaps between the ideal simulated experimental environment and the physical mobile environment. We try to list the differences and their possible impacts to the 2S-DORA as follows.

1. In a physical mobile environment, some mobile users are likely to lose their connections to the wireless network. The disconnection will result in some useless requests and affect the quality of the joint optimal solution to the MCDCOP.
2. In a physical mobile environment, some service providers may not provide their services on schedule. Such service delays though are not considered in the simulated environment, this kind of exceptions can be handled by the 2S-DORA.
3. In a physical mobile environment, some users will not help others even though they have nothing to loss. The selfish mobile users may lower down the quality of the joint optimal solution.
4. In a physical mobile environment, mobile users' satisfaction and decision models may not be as simple as we formulate. Since the 2S-DORA helps all mobile users pursue and improve their personal objectives, the 2S-DORA can perform well even if mobile users' satisfaction and decision models are complicated and distinguishing.
5. In a physical mobile environment, most service providers charge for their services. The service fees are neglected to simplify the experiments. The SPA+2S-DORA can still perform well if the service charges are considered as the expenses of mobile users' enjoyments.

Chapter 9 Conclusion and Future Research

This chapter makes conclusions in Section 9.1 and suggests future research direction in Section 9.2.

9.1 Conclusion

The advance of communication technologies stimulates the growth of mobile computing. We explore and analyze the Mobile Users Coordination Problem (MUCP) that arises in the mobile environment. We expect that the problem will occur more and more frequently in the near future. We concentrate on resolving the conflict problem by coordinating users' activities. We formulate the problem as a multi-objective context-dependent DCOP (MCDCOP). We propose the integrated multi-agent systems SPA and a problem-solving approach 2S-DORA to address the MCDCOP. We evaluate the performance of the SPA+2S-DORA by carried out experiments on a traveling backpacker problem, which is an extension of the MUCP. The experimental results show that the 2S-DORA can effectively solve the MUCP.

Table 9.1 summarizes the characteristics of the MCDCOP and lists the abilities of SPA+2S-DORA to handle the MCDCOP.

Table 9.1 Characteristics of MCDCOP and the abilities of SPA+2S-DORA to handle the MCDCOP

Characteristics of MCDCOP	Abilities of SPA+2S-DORA
Distributed optimization	Obtaining optimal solutions subject to the shared constraints in a distributed environment by using physical agents to communicate necessary information to other agents.
Multi-objective optimization /joint optimal solution	Interoperating with other SPA+2S-DORAs to achieve a joint optimum solution by first pursuing personal optimization and then cooperatively improving the optimization with others.

Characteristics of MCDCOP	Abilities of SPA+2S-DORA
Context-dependent optimization	Gaining context-dependent optimization by re-planning personal policies and making continuous improvement.
Subject to personal and shared constraints	Analyzing and communicating with others iteratively to get rid of infeasible solutions which violate personal and shared constraints.

The experimental results in Chapter 8 draw the following important conclusions.

1. The 2S-DORA can effectively help mobile users plan and improve their joint activity schedules.
2. If mobile users adopt the SPA+2S-DORA embedded mobile devices, the tourist attractions' utilization rates will significantly raise. The users' satisfactions will also significantly increase.
3. In the distributed environment, with the assistance of SPA agent systems, the 2S-DORA performs as well as that in the centralized environment.
4. In a busy season, the more the SPA+2S-DORA users, the more possibility that the SPA+2S-DORA users will benefit from it to gain higher expected satisfactions.
5. In a slack season, users with SPA+2S-DORA gain insignificant advantages over those without any mobile devices.
6. The SPA+2S-DORA can effectively help mobile users adjust their schedules and resolve conflicts that follow the context variations and exceptions occurred in the mobile environment.

Our theoretical and practical contributions are summarized as follows. In the theoretical aspect:

1. We investigate the MUCP, extract its characteristics and formulate it into a new problem, the MCDCOP.
2. We propose a novel multi-agent framework SPA, which integrates physical

and simulated agents to enhance a user's sensory, analyzing, reasoning and social abilities. The SPA can support real time and online decision makings in a highly dynamic and complicated environment.

3. We survey and analyze the problem-solving techniques that may be applied to solve the MCDCOP, such as OptAPO, DPOP, ADOPT and MCA, and concludes that a new intelligent technique is required.
4. We develop a new problem-solving technique 2S-DORA, which can successfully solve the MCDCOP to maintain the solution optimality in the highly dynamic and complicated mobile environment.
5. We draw three heuristics for the MCDCOP to search for joint optimal solution more efficiently.
6. We propose two metrics, satisfactions of mobile users and capacity utilization rates of service providers, to evaluate the performance of a problem-solving technique that is applied to solve the MCDCOP.

In the practical aspect:

1. We employ JADE physical agent systems and Swarm simulated agent systems to implement SPA.
2. We propose a flexible coordination mechanism for mobile users in a highly dynamic environment to coordinate with each other to resolve conflicts.
3. We offer a systematic procedure for distributed mobile users to develop their reservation exchange schemes to improve their activity schedules.
4. We specify a reservation exchange protocol, defines performative and communication ontology and rules for mobile users to coordinate with the others.
5. We define state transition rules to regulate mobile users' behaviors to avoid data inconsistencies during coordination.
6. We develop SPA+2S-DORA to help mobile users improve their schedules and resolve their conflicts that follow the context variations and exceptions occurred in the mobile environment. The service providers in the mobile

environment also benefits from users' adoption of the SPA+2S-DORA.

9.2 Future Research Direction

We suggest some potential research directions. First, add incentive mechanism into the 2S-DORA to motivate mobile users to help other users. For example, the one who helps other mobile users more often will have higher priority to ask for help or have rewards as feedback.

Second, analyze the casual relations of the 2S-DORA parameters to find the optimal combination of the parameters to increase the 2S-DORA's efficiencies under certain situations. The parameters can be the maximum size of the coordination network and the maximum frequency that a mobile user is allowed to improve his/her policy. Taguchi method can be an experimental approach to performing the analysis.

Third, design a fee charging system to prevent mobile users to endlessly try their better policies. This fee charging system can avoid useless communication in the mobile environment and save the wireless communication resources.

Fourth, explore smarter ways for large-sized problems to help mobile users efficiently improve their policies. In the mobile environment, not annoying the mobile users' happiness and enjoyments are imperative. Therefore, every improvement should be carried out unconsciously in a period as short as possible.

Fifth, employ the SPA+2S-DORA to a larger problem to check its performance, e.g., a problem in which 50,000 backpackers are traveling in a mobile city. Moreover, broaden the applications of SPA+2S-DORA, such as coordinating the visits of businesspeople to the booths of a business show and coordinating the facility usages of the tourists in a theme park.

Sixth, take other possible exceptions into consideration, such as the disconnection of wireless communication, and loose the limitations described in Chapter 1, to make the SPA+2S-DORA more applicable and practical.

Seventh, measure how far or how near the joint optimal solution, obtained by the SPA+2S-DORA, approaches the Pareto optimal solution to evaluate the quality of the solution.

Finally, evaluate the performance of SPA+2S-DORA in different `REQUEST` message sending modes, *e.g.*, in unicast mode, multicast mode, or broadcast mode. Moreover, investigate which message sending mode will perform best under what conditions.

Reference

Ahmad, N. (2004). The humanoid Robot Cog. *Crossroads, 10*(2), pp.3-3.

Ali, A., & Kennington, J. (1986). The Asymmetric m-Traveling Salesmen Problem: a Duality Based Branch-and-Bound Algorithm. *Discrete Applied Mathematics*, pp.259–276.

Bankston, J. B., & Harnett, R. M. (2000). An heuristic algorithm for a multi-product, single machine capacitated production scheduling problem *Computers & Operations Research, 27*(1), pp. 77-92.

Bantz, D. F., Bisdikian, C., Challener, D., Karidis, J. P., Mastrianni, S., Mohindra, A., . . . Vanover, M. (2003). Autonomic personal computing. *IBM Systems Journal, 42*(1), pp.165-176.

Bektas, T. (2006). The Multiple Traveling Salesman Problem: an Overview of Formulations and Solution Procedures. *The international journal of management science*, pp. 209-219.

Bellmore, M., & Hong, S. (1974a). Transformation of multi salesmen problem to the standard traveling salesman problem. *Journal of Association for Computing Machinery, 21*, pp.500-504.

Bellmore, M., & Hong, S. (1974b). Transformation of multisalesmen problem to the standard traveling salesman problem. *Journal of Association for Computing Machinery, 21*, pp.500-504.

Bond, A. H., & Gasser, L. (1988). *Readings in Distributed Artificial Intelligence*. San Mateo, CA.: Morgan Kaufman Publishers.

Bowring, E., Tambe, M., & Yokoo, M. (2005). *Distributed Multi-Criteria Coordination in Multi-Agent Systems.* Paper presented at the Workshop on Declarative Agent Languages and Technologies at the Fourth International Joint Conference on Agents and Multiagent Systems (DALT-05), Utrecht, Netherlands.

Bui, L. T., Abbass, H. A., & Essam, D. (2006). *Local Models: An Approach to Distributed Multiobjective Optimization* (TR-ALAR-200601002). Retrieved from

Choe, Y. (2014). *Why do travellers change their trip? Effects of context, individual, and information factors.* Paper presented at the Information and Communication Technologies in Tourism 2014 Dublin, Ireland.

Clement, M., Okimoto, T., Ribeiro, T., & Inoue, K. (2013). Model and algorithm for dynamic multi-objective distributed optimization *PRIMA 2013: Principles and Practice of Multi-Agent Systems* (pp. 413-420): Springer.

Davidsson, P. (2002). Agent Based Social Simulation: A Computer Science View. . *Journal of Artificial Societies and Social Simulation, 5*(1). Retrieved from

Delle Fave, F. M., Stranders, R., Rogers, A., & Jennings, N. R. (2011). *Bounded decentralised coordination over multiple objectives.* Paper presented at the The 10th International Conference on Autonomous Agents and Multiagent Systems (AAMSA 2011), Taipei, Taiwan.

Dey, A. K., & Abowd, G. D. (1999). *Towards a Better Understanding of Context and Context Awareness.* Paper presented at the 1st International Symposium on Handheld and Ubiquitous Computing (HUC'99), Karlsruhe, Germany.

Durfee, E. H., & Lesser, V. (1989). *Negotiating Task Decomposition and Allocation Using Partial Global Planning* (Vol. 2). San Francisco, Calif.: Morgan Kaufmann.

Feldmann, M., & Biskup, D. (2003). Single-machine scheduling for minimizing earliness and tardiness penalties by meta-heuristic approaches *Computers and Industrial Engineering, 44*(2), pp.307-323.

Fogel, D. (1990). *A parallel processing approach to a multiple traveling salesman problem using evolutionary programming.* Paper presented at the 4th annual symposium on parallel processing, Fullerton, CA.

Foner, L. N. (Producer). (1993, http://foner.www.media.mit.edu/people/foner/Reports/Julia/Agents--Julia.pdf). What's an Agent, Anyway? A Sociological Case Study.

Gajski, D. D., & Ramachandran, L. (1994). Introduction to High-Level Synthesis. *IEEE Design & Test of Computers, 11*(4), 44-54.

Ganek, A. G., & Corbi, T. A. (2003). The Dawning of the Autonomic Computing Era. *IBM Systems Journal, 42*(1), pp.5-18.

Gilbert, K., & Hofstra, R. (1992). A new multiperiod multiple traveling salesman problem with heuristic and application to a scheduling problem. *Decision Sciences, 23*, 250–259.

Goldstein, M. (1990). *Self-organizing feature maps for the multiple traveling salesmen problem.* Paper presented at the IEEE international conference on neural network, San Diego, CA.

Gromicho, J., Paixão, J., & Branco, I. (1992). *Exact Solution of Multiple Traveling Salesman Problems.*

Gruber, T. (1993). A translation approach to portable ontologies. *Knowledge Acquisition, 5*(2), pp. 199-220.

GuoXing, Y. (1995). Transformation of multidepot multisalesmen problem to the standard traveling salesman problem. *Journal of Operational Research, 81*, pp.557-560.

Gutierrez, P., & Meseguer, P. (2010). *Saving redundant messages in BnB-ADOPT.* Paper presented at the Twenty-Fourth AAAI Conference on Artificial Intelligence (AAAI-10), Georgia, USA.

Hall, A., & Taubig, H. (2003). *Comparing push and pull-based broadcasting.* Paper presented at the Second International Workshop on Experimental and Efficient Algorithms, Monte Verità, Ascona, Switzerland.

Hayes-Roth, B. (1995). An Architecture for Adaptive Intelligent Systems. *Artificial Intelligence: Special Issue on Agents and Interactivity, 72*, pp.329-365.

Hong, S., & Padberg, M. (1977). A note on the symmetric multiple traveling salesman problem with fixed charges. *Operations Research, 25*(5), pp.871–874.

Hsu, C., Tsai, M., & Chen, W. (1991). A study of feature-mapped approach to the multiple travelling salesmen problem. *IEEE International Symposium on Circuits and Systems, 3*, pp.1589-1592.

Hwang, Y.-H., & Fesenmaier, D. R. (2011). Unplanned tourist attraction visits by travellers. *Tourism Geographies - An International Journal of Tourism Space, Place and Environment, 13*(3), 398-416.

Ishiguro, H. (2002). *Toward interactive humanoid robots: a constructive approach to developing intelligent robots*. Paper presented at the first international joint conference on Autonomous agents and multiagent systems.

Jennings, N. R., Sycara, K., & Wooldridge., M. (1998). A roadmap of agent research and development. . *Autonomous Agents and Multi-Agent Systems, 1*, 7-38.

Jonker, R., & Volgenant, T. (1988). An improved transformation of the symmetric multiple traveling salesman problem. *Operations Research, 36*(1), pp.163-167.

Kaiser, G., Gross, P., Kc, G., Parekh, J., & Valetto, G. (2002). *An approach to autonomizing legacy systems*. Paper presented at the ACM Workshop on Self-Healing, Adaptive and self-MANaged Systems (SHAMAN), New York City.

Kephart, J. O., & Chess, D. M. (2003). The Vision of Autonomic Computing. *IEEE Computer, 36*(1), pp.41-50.

Kramer, R., Modsching, M., Hagen, K. T., & Gretzel, U. (2007). *Behavioural impacts of mobile tour guides*. Paper presented at the Information and Communication Technologies in Tourism, Vienna, Ljubljana, Slovenia.

Krause, S., Morais, d. A. S. F., Magedanz, T., PopescuZeletin, R., Falsarella, O. M., & Mendez, C. R. A. (1997). *MAGNA -- A DPE-Based Platform for Mobile Agents in Electronic Service Markets*. Paper presented at the Third International Symposium on Autonomous Decentralized Systems.

Laporte, G., & Nobert, Y. (1980). A Cutting Planes Algorithm for the m-Salesmen Problem. *Journal of the Operational Research Society*(31), pp.1017–1023.

Laporte, G., Nobert, Y., & Taillefer, S. (1988). Solving a family of multi-depot vehicle routing and location-routing problems. *Transportation Science, 22*(3), pp.161-172.

Lee, K. K., Yu, M., & Xu, Y. (2003). *Modeling of human walking trajectories for surveillance*. Paper presented at the Intelligent Robots and Systems, 2003. (IROS 2003).

Lin, F.-r., & Lin, S.-m. (2006). Enhancing the Supply Chain Performance by Integrating Simulated and Physical Agents into Organizational Information Systems. *Journal of Artificial Societies and Social Simulation, 9*(4).

Liu, J., & Yao, C. (2004). Rational competition and cooperation in ubiquitous agent communities. *Knowledge-Based Systems, 17*(5-6), pp. 189-200.

Liu, S. Q., Ong, H. L., & Ng, K. M. (2005). Metaheuristics for minimizing the makespan of the dynamic shop scheduling problem *Advances in Engineering Software, 36*(3), pp. 199-205.

Luger, G. F., & Stubblefield, W. A. (1997). *Artificial Intelligence: Structures and Strategies for Complex Problem Solving* (3rd ed.). Boston, MA, USA Addison-Wesley Longman Publishing Co., Inc. .

Luna, F., & Stefansson, B. (2000). *Economic Simulation in Swarm: Agent-based Modeling and Object Oriented Programming*. Boston: Kluwer Academic Publishers.

Maes, P. (1995). Artificial life meets entertainment: life like autonomous agents. *Communications of the ACM, 38*(11), pp. 108-114.

Mailler, R., & Lesser, V. (2004). *Solving Distributed Constraint Optimization Problems Using Cooperative Mediation.* Paper presented at the Third International Joint Conference on Autonomous Agents and Multiagent Systems.

Malone, T. W., & Crowston, K. (1994). The Interdisciplinary Study of Coordination. *ACM Computing Survey, 26*(1).

Matossian, V., & Parashar, M. (2003). *Autonomic Optimization of an Oil Reservoir using Decentralized Services.* Paper presented at the 1st International Workshop on Heterogeneous and Adaptive Computing-- Challenges for Large Applications in Distributed Environments (CLADE 2003), Seattle, WA, USA.

Minar, N., Burkhart, R., Langton, C., & Askenazi, M. (Producer). (1996, http://www.swarm.org). The Swarm simulation system: a toolkit for building multi-agent simulations.

Mingozzi, A., Maniezzo, V., Ricciardelli, S., & Bianco, L. (1998). An Exact

Algorithm for the Resource-Constrained Project Scheduling Problem Based on a New Mathematical Formulation. *44*(5), pp. 714 - 729.

Modares, A., Somhom, S., & Enkawa, T. (1999). A self-organizing neural network approach for multiple traveling salesman and vehicle routing problems. *International Transactions in Operational Research, 6*, pp.591-606.

Modi, P. J., Shen, W. M., Tambe, M., Yokoo, M., & Journal, A. I. (2005). ADOPT: Asynchronous distributed constraint optimization with quality guarantees. *Artificial Intelligence Journal, 161*, pp.149–180.

Mokotoff, E. (2004). An exact algorithm for the identical parallel machine scheduling problem. *European Journal of Operational Research, 152*(3), pp. 758-769.

Netzer, A., Grubshtein, A., & Meisels, A. (2012). Concurrent forward bounding for distributed constraint optimization problems. *Artificial Intelligence, 193*, 186-216. doi:10.1016/j.artint.2012.09.002

Niemelä, E., & Latvakoski, J. (2004). *Survey of requirements and solutions for ubiquitous software.* Paper presented at the 3rd international conference on Mobile and ubiquitous multimedia

O'Grady, M. J., & O'Hare, G. M. P. (2005). Mobile devices and intelligent agents: towards a new generation of applications and services. *Information Sciences, 171*, 335-353.

Okimoto, T., Clement, M., & Inoue, K. (2013). *AOF-based algorithm for dynamic multi-objective distributed constraint optimization.* Paper presented at the The 7th Multi-Disciplinary International Workshop on Artificial Intelligence (MIWAI'13), Krabi, Thailand.

Okimoto, T., Schwind, N., Clement, M., & Inoue, K. (2014). *Lp-norm based algorithm for multi-objective distributed constraint optimization.* Paper presented at the The 2014 International Conference on Autonomous Agents and Multi-agent Systems, Paris, France.

Oliveira, E., Fischer, K., & Stepankova, O. (1999). Multi-agent systems: Which research for which applications. *Journal of Robotics and Autonomous Systems,*

27(1-2), pp. 91-106.

Petcu, A., & Faltings, B. (2005). *A scalable method for multiagent constraint optimization.* Paper presented at the 19th International Joint Conference on Artificial Intelligence, Edinburgh, Scotland.

Pinedo, M. (1995). *Scheduling: Theory, Algorithms, and Systems*. Englewood Cliffs, NJ: Prentice Hall.

Potvin, J., Lapalme, G., & Rousseau, J. (1989). A generalized k-opt exchange procedure for the MTSP. *Information Fusion, 27*(4), pp.474-481.

Rajendran, C. (1995). Heuristics for scheduling in flowshop with multiple objectives. *European Journal of Operational Research, 82*(3), pp. 540-555.

Rao, M. (1980). A note on the multiple traveling salesman problem. *Operations Research, 28*(3), pp.628-632.

Rao, S. (1991). *Optimization theory and application*. New Delhi: Wiley Eastern Limited.

Richards, G., & Wilson, J. (2004). *The global nomad :backpacker travel in theory and practice.* Clevedon England: Buffalo N.Y.

Russell, J., & Norvig, P. (2003). *Artificial Intelligence: A Modern Approach* (2nd edition ed.): Prentice Hall.

Russell, R. (1977). An effective heuristic for the m-tour traveling salesman problem with some side conditions. *Operations Research, 25*(3), pp.517–524.

Sandholm, T. W. (1996). *Negotiation among Self-Interested Computationally Limited Agents.* (PhD), University of Massachusetts, Amherst.

Sashima, A., Izumi, N., & Kurumatani, K. (2004). *Bridging Coordination Gaps between Devices, Services, and Humans in Ubiquitous Computing.* Paper presented at the International Workshop on Agents for Ubiquitous Computing, 3rd International Joint Conference on Autonomous Agents and Multi Agent Systems.

Sofge, D., Schultz, A., & DeJong, K. (2002). Evolutionary computational approaches to solving the multiple traveling salesman problem using a neighborhood attractor schema. *Lecture notes in computer science*, pp.151-160.

Somhom, S., Modares, A., & Enkawa, T. (1999). Competition-based neural network for the multiple traveling salesmen problem with minmax objective. *Computers and Operations Research, 26*(4), pp.395-407.

Song, C., Lee, K., & Lee, W. D. (2003). *Extended simulated annealing for augmented TSP and multi-salesmen TSP.* Paper presented at the the international joint conference on neural networks.

T'Kindt, V., & Billaut, J.-C. (2002). Multicriteria Scheduling Problems. In M. Ehrgot & X. Gandibleux (Eds.), *Multiple Criteria Optimization: State of the Art Annotated Bibliographic Surveys* (1 ed., pp. 520). Dordrecht: Kluwer Academic.

T'kindt, V., & Billaut, J.-C. (2006). Introduction to Scheduling *Multicriteria Scheduling: Theory, Models and Algorithms* (2 ed., pp. p8, p15). Berlin: Springer.

Tafat, A., Courant, M., & Hirsbrunner, B. (2005). *Coordination models, languages and applications (CM): Implicit environment-based coordination in pervasive computing.* Paper presented at the 2005 ACM symposium on Applied computing

Tang, L., Liu, J., Rong, A., & Yang, Z. (2000). A multiple traveling salesman problem model for hot rolling scheduling in Shangai Baoshan Iron & Steel Company. *European Journal of Operational Research, 124*, pp.267-282.

Wacholder, E., Han, J., & Mann, R. (1989). A neural network algorithm for the multiple traveling salesmen problem. *Biology in Cybernetics, 61*, pp.11-19.

Wang, D., Park, S., & Fesenmaier, D. R. (2012). The role of smartphones in mediating the touristic experience. *Journal of Travel Research, 51*, 371-387.

Wang, J. F. (2001). *Distributed multi-criteria optimization using GAs and game theory and related applications to high lift CFD problems in aerodynamics.* (Ph.D), University of Paris France.

Weidmann, N. B., & Girardin, L. (2005). Technical note: evaluating java development kits for agent-based modeling. *Journal of Artificial Societies and Social Simulation, 8*(2). Retrieved from

Weiser, M. (1991). The Computer for the Twenty-First Century. *Scientific American*, pp. 94-104.

Weiss, G. (1999). *Multiagent systems: a modern approach to distributed artificial intelligence*. London, England: MIT Press.

Wittner, O., Heegaard, P. E., & Helvik, B. E. (2002). *Swarm Based Distributed Search in the AMIGOS Environment* (ISSN 1503-4097). Retrieved from

Wolter, R. (2013). Network-Embedded Management and Applications. In A. Clemm & R. Wolter (Eds.), *Motivation: The Dawn of the Age of Network-Embedded Applications* (pp. 23-57). New York: Springer.

Wooldridge, M., & Jennings, N. R. (1995). Agent theories, architectures, and languages: a survey. In M. Wooldridge & J. N.R. (Eds.), *Intelligent Agents* (pp. pp. 1-22): Berlin: Springer-Verlag.

Yeoh, W., Felner, A., & Koenig, S. (2008). *BnB-ADOPT: An asynchronous branch-and-bound DCOP algorithm.* Paper presented at the The 7th international joint conference on Autonomous agents and multiagent systems (AAMAS '08), Estoril, Portugal.

Yeoh, W., Varakantham, P., Sun, X., & Koenig, S. (2011). *Incremental DCOP search algorithms for solving dynamic DCOPs.* Paper presented at the The 10th International Conference on Autonomous Agents and Multiagent Systems (AAMAS 2011), Taipei, Taiwan.

Yu, Z., Jinhai, L., Guochang, G., Rubo, Z., & Haiyan, Y. (2002). An Implementation of Evolutionary Computation for Path Planning of Cooperative Mobile Robots. *4th world congress on intelligent control and automation, 3*, pp.1798-1802.

Zhang, T., Gruver, W., & Smith, M. (1999). *Team Scheduling by Genetic Search.*

FSC www.fsc.org
MIX
Papier aus verantwortungsvollen Quellen
Paper from responsible sources
FSC® C105338

Printed by Books on Demand GmbH, Norderstedt / Germany